BLAZING YOUR OWN TRAIL

Blazing Your Own Trail

Faith, Focus, and Forward Momentum in Leadership

Kiki Baker Barnes, PhD

©2025 All Rights Reserved. No portion of this book may be reproduced, stored in a retrieval system, or transmitted in any form or by any means—electronic, mechanical, photocopy, recording, scanning, or other—except for brief quotations in critical reviews or articles without the prior permission of the author.

Published by Game Changer Publishing

Paperback ISBN: 978-1-965653-42-5

Hardcover ISBN: 978-1-965653-43-2

Digital ISBN: 978-1-965653-44-9

www.GameChangerPublishing.com

DEDICATION

This book is dedicated to all of the young people I have had the privilege to lead throughout my career. Thank you for trusting me.

University of Louisiana at Lafayette Women's Basketball Teams 1997-1999

Southern University at Shreveport Women's Basketball, Cheer, and Jazzy Jagz Teams 2000-2002

Frank Phillips College Women's Basketball Team 2002-2003

Dillard University Women's Basketball Teams 2005-2013

Dillard University Bleu Crew and Game Day Management Team 2006- 2022

So You Want A Career in Athletics™ Community

READ THIS FIRST

Just to say thanks for buying and reading my book,
I would like to give you a free gift:

Trailblazing Action Plan:
A Step-by-Step Guide to Blazing Your Own Trail

Scan the QR Code Here:

BLAZING YOUR OWN TRAIL

FAITH, FOCUS, AND FORWARD MOMENTUM IN LEADERSHIP

KIKI BAKER BARNES

www.GameChangerPublishing.com

FOREWORD

Over the course of my career, I have met a lot of people who could articulate big dreams and goals. They were excited about them and could speak passionately about them as well. But they all missed one key ingredient. They didn't want to do what was required to achieve their dreams. Journalist Roland Martin often says this on his show that he meets people who say they want to do what he does, but they don't really want to do everything he does.

When I met Dr. Kiki Baker Barnes in 2012 as I joined the team at Dillard University, it was evident early on that this was someone who had big dreams and goals, and not only did she strategize about how to achieve them, but she also did the work. Being an athlete, she understood hard work, competition, and what winning looks like. Just like any superstar athlete who continues to practice their craft, Dr. Barnes, over the course of her career, has practiced being an exceptional athletic administrator.

Dillard University is a small, private, historically Black institution. Being in a small athletic association, she knew there was no illusion that resources would flow like we see with big-time college sports. She had to think about ways to support her program, including fundraising events with a vision of raising significant resources. She

FOREWORD

imagined game day experiences that would draw not only students but community leaders to campus to root for our teams. She even raised the profile of our signature rivalry basketball games with celebrity performances during halftime.

As an athletics director, her winning attitude and work ethic was truly contagious. I know that sounds like a worn cliché, but if you believe in the law of attraction, you know that dynamic people can get dynamic people to join their team. When I first arrived at Dillard, our men's basketball program was in shambles, winning just a few games. Dr. Barnes was able to attract a very seasoned coach who came in saying he was going to win championships. A lot of that was in his DNA, but he could see that with Dr. Barnes as the leader, his passion would easily come to life. He immediately started winning both conference regular season and tournament championships.

We saw the same with a new track and field coach, who came in confident, put in the work, and immediately won championships as well. Finally, as I was closing out my last year at Dillard we started a baseball program. I bet you can guess what happened their first season- a conference championship.

What makes her legacy even greater is the fact that she was responsible for rebuilding athletics as the institution literally rebuilt after Hurricane Katrina. She didn't simply have to find coaches and players; she had to help oversee the rebuilding of facilities for the program. During my tenure, we had to evacuate the campus for two hurricanes, so as the AD she had to plan for the fall sports to stay safe as well as continue their seasons even if that meant operating from a sister institution.

She brings a unique mix of organization, vision, planning, relationship building, and competitiveness, skills that I believe can be useful for anyone in our professional lives, and maybe to a degree personally. She wants to be the best but wants to do it in a way that is ethical. You immediately learn that she operates from a strong sense of faith and family and that she cares for the students and their families, her colleagues, and her community.

The late writer E. Lynn Harris once told me after a speech he gave in Norfolk, Virginia, when I worked at Old Dominion University, that

FOREWORD

the key to life is to find something you love doing and that you would do for free and then find a way to get paid to do it. Dr. Barnes LOVES athletics. She loves the competition. She loves creating dynamic game day experiences. She loves introducing young women to the possibility of careers in athletics. She loves encouraging and inspiring people. When you have a leader like this, you can experience lots of success. You are also able to properly put into perspective those times when things don't work out like you'd hoped. Sure, she has had her share of disappointments, but she is able to reflect on those experiences and then reposition herself to move forward.

This book is an opportunity for the reader to gain some insight into not just who she is as a person, but how she processes the world. A role model for so many, she is sharing through this book lessons she has learned over time in hopes that the readers might be able to turn those ideas into opportunities for themselves.

I have been fortunate to hire some tremendously talented people during my career and have watched them go on and do amazing things. Kiki Baker Barnes was not one of them. She was a gift that Dillard already had, and I am glad I have enough sense to know a superstar when I see one. All I had to do was make sure she knew that I knew she was a superstar and that she had free range to fully be herself.

And then I just watched the magic happen.

–Walter M. Kimbrough, PhD
7th president, Dillard University

CONTENTS

INTRODUCTION	xv

PART 1
FUNDAMENTALS OF BLAZING YOUR OWN TRAIL

Chapter 1 *FAITH*	3
Chapter 2 *FOCUS*	17
Chapter 3 *FORWARD MOMENTUM*	27

PART 2
CHALLENGES OF BLAZING YOUR OWN TRAIL

Chapter 4 *MANAGING TRANSITION*	41
Chapter 5 *EMBRACING COMPETITION AND PREPARATION*	57

PART 3
CATALYST TO BLAZING YOUR OWN TRAIL

Chapter 6 *FORESIGHT AND FAILURE*	69

PART 4
BENEFITS OF BLAZING YOUR OWN TRAIL

Chapter 7 *THE PATH REVEALED*	83
Chapter 8 *MY PURPOSE REALIZED*	93
CONCLUSION: A NEW BEGINNING	105
THANK YOU	109

INTRODUCTION

My early introduction to sports was through cheerleading, which was my first love. I was exposed to basketball and baseball because my dad was a former athlete who played some college baseball and basketball, and I had other family members who played sports. My mom was a musician, and she didn't participate in any sports. But I remember my first opportunity to play sports was going to our local recreational park to play "biddy basketball," as they called it. Parents would sign you up, and they would put you on a team to play games over a period of six weeks or so. They weren't really teaching us the fundamentals at the time. It was honestly just an opportunity to have fun, connect with other kids, and stay healthy and active.

I was born in 1975, three years after the passage of Title IX, and there was a boom in participation numbers for young girls competing in sports. A number of initiatives promoted opportunities for young girls to participate in sports. This was important to my trajectory as a person who has now spent her entire career working in sports and higher education. The lessons that I plan to share throughout this book are lessons that I learned as early as fifth grade all the way through high school.

I like to talk about this time in my life because I think there are

INTRODUCTION

misconceptions about when development and learning actually happen, and when you can start to develop the skills, learn your purpose, and connect with your intuition to help you grow. When we are young, learning often involves a teacher or some authority figure telling us what to do and providing direction. Utilizing curriculum and instruction, the teacher provides foundational knowledge to aid both our educational and personal development. While this method is the standard for teaching and learning, it is not the only way. I've gone from being taught how to memorize an Easter speech as a kid to writing and delivering a university commencement address, which is an amazing transformation in itself.

As I've had the opportunity to reflect on my life, I've realized that life has also been teaching and guiding me since I was old enough to have cognition. Learning fueled my curiosity to know more, and I began to have my own goals and desires. I remember watching the Olympics and seeing Flo-Jo and Jackie Joyner-Kersee and thinking, *I would love to have the opportunity to be one of those ladies and be a superstar track athlete.* I remember watching the Dallas Cowboy cheerleaders and wanting to be one of those famous cowgirl cheerleaders. I remember watching the local junior high school cheerleading squad and thinking, *Wow, I have a desire to achieve these goals,* but I needed to figure out how to get the skills necessary to make it happen. There were valuable lessons learned in those formative years that have contributed to my personal success, and I am excited to share them with you. My desire is that from my journey, you will learn how to examine your own life experiences—what's happening internally (within you) and externally (around you)—through reflection and discernment to inform your decision-making process.

One thing I've learned is that you can never know everything—it's not possible. It's similar to algebra, which was one of my favorite subjects in high school. One of the first formulas I learned was linear equations, where the goal is to solve for X. In order to solve for X, you have to take the variables you do know in order to assist you with solving for what you don't know. In the life equation, the variables you do know are your experiences and knowledge. It's a great metaphor for life in general and what it feels like to *blaze your own trail*. A ques-

INTRODUCTION

tion I often get asked is: How do I know which way to go, which person I should listen to, or what piece of knowledge will help me solve the problem I have at this point in my life? Well, I have written this book to give you a formula to solve for X in your life as you look to discover your own path.

So, who is this book for?

This book is for anyone who has ever felt lost in life's transitions, those searching for their purpose, and those determined to lead with integrity and courage. Whether you're at the beginning of your career, facing a major life transition, or simply seeking inspiration, this book is for you. The stories, lessons, and insights shared here are meant to encourage you to embrace the unknown, trust in your abilities, and stay true to your path.

This is an opportunity to examine the path of someone very similar —a young woman who was excited about life, had dreams and aspirations, and woke up every day trying to solve for X. This is a book for those looking to develop courage and confidence, understand how to take the necessary steps toward reaching their goals or finding their purpose, and, more importantly, become the best version of themselves.

Why listen to me? I am an award-winning college sports executive with over 28 years of experience successfully leading people and organizations. I've been sought out to provide my expertise on leadership in both the sports industry and higher education in national media outlets such as TBS, NPR, *Essence Magazine*, *Sports Illustrated*, *Andscape*, *Black Enterprise*, *TheGRIO*, *Diverse Issues in Higher Education*, and *Women in Higher Education*. I've received numerous academic and athletic awards, including the Nell Jackson Nike Executive of the Year Award (2021) and Administrator of the Year (2015), presented by Women Leaders in Sports (WLS), Trailblazer Award (2021) presented by the Higher Education Leadership Foundation (HELF), Under Armour Athletic Director of the Year, presented by National Association of College Directors of Athletics (NACDA), and the Girl Scout Woman of Distinction Award. It has been an honor to be called on and seen as an advisor, someone people can trust to provide sound counsel

INTRODUCTION

on addressing issues within the industry and within colleges and universities.

What you can expect from this book is more in-depth information on my personal journey of self-discovery, learning to make sense of how bad experiences and failures informed my rise to success, and my ability to achieve the goals I had set for myself—even some things that I didn't anticipate happening. Life is a journey filled with transitions, challenges, and unexpected turns. From a young age, I knew that my path would be anything but ordinary, but I never imagined the twists and turns that would shape it. This book is the culmination of years of experience, hard-earned lessons, and wisdom gained from navigating the complexities of life, leadership, and purpose.

The idea of blazing your own trail has always resonated with me. It's about more than just achieving success; it's about finding your true purpose, aligning your actions with your values, and embracing the journey with all its ups and downs. As I look back on my life, I realize that every challenge, every failure, and every victory prepared me for something greater. This book is my attempt to share that journey with you, not as a roadmap, but as a guide to help you navigate your own path.

THE BLIND EXCHANGE FRAMEWORK

At the core of this book is the Blind Exchange Framework, a concept born out of my experiences as an athlete and a leader. The Blind Exchange represents the moments in life when we must rely on faith, focus, and forward momentum—often without seeing the full picture. It's about trusting the process, even when the outcome is uncertain, and moving forward with conviction. This framework has guided me through some of the most challenging times in my life, and it's my hope that it will offer you the same clarity and strength as you navigate your own journey.

In the chapters that follow, I'll take you through the pivotal moments of my life, from the early days of discovering my passion for sports to the challenges of leadership in the professional world. Each chapter is filled with stories of failure and triumph, moments of doubt

INTRODUCTION

and clarity, and the lessons learned along the way. You'll see how the principles of the Blind Exchange Framework—faith, focus, and forward momentum—have shaped my decisions and guided me through the many transitions I've faced.

This book is not just about my journey; it's about the universal experiences that we all share as we strive to find our way in the world. It's about the power of perseverance, the importance of staying true to your values, and the courage it takes to step into the unknown. As you read, I encourage you to reflect on your own journey, think about the lessons you've learned, and consider how you can apply the principles of the Blind Exchange Framework in your own life. My hope is that this book will serve as a companion on your journey, offering guidance, encouragement, and inspiration as you blaze your own trail.

Let's begin this journey together.

PART 1

FUNDAMENTALS OF BLAZING YOUR OWN TRAIL

1
FAITH

THE ROLE OF FAITH IN MY LIFE

I grew up in Minden, Louisiana, a small town with a population of just over 12,000. Nestled in the northwest corner of the state in Webster Parish, Minden was a place where faith and community were deeply intertwined. Louisiana is unique in that it uses the term "parish" instead of "county"—a nod to its French and Roman Catholic roots. We didn't view the cities in in Webster Parish as just geographical boundaries; they were communities bound together by shared beliefs and values.

Minden was 53% Black and 43% white, but like many small towns in the Deep South, positions of power and authority were predominantly held by white people. Neighborhoods were largely segregated, with Highway 79—also known as Main Street—marking the dividing line. On the south side of Main Street lived the majority of Black families, while the north side was mostly white. Despite these divisions, faith was the thread that held the community together. It was the foundation upon which everything else was built.

My family was no different. My mother, Linda, was a music teacher at Forest Hill Elementary School in Shreveport, 41 miles away from Minden.

My father, Bobby, was a bricklayer. The nature of his work was unpredictable and project-based, but his faith and work ethic were constants. My grandparents on both sides were also hardworking individuals whose lives revolved around their faith and family. My grandmother, Grandy (Bertha Lee Hunter), worked as a maid and a cafeteria lady, Grandma Beesie (Laura Baker) worked as a maid, and my grandfather, Paw Paw (Fulton Hunter), labored at the local lumber supply company. For all of them, faith was the quiet force that guided their daily lives.

Growing up, my days were filled with the sounds of gospel music, starting with what my mother played during our 41-minute drive to Forest Hill Elementary School in Shreveport, LA, each morning. You see, my mom wasn't just a music teacher; she was a church musician, a soloist, and a woman whose life was defined by her faith. She was the first Black woman to compete in the Miss Minden pageant (in 1969), and she went on to graduate from Grambling State University, making her the first of her siblings to graduate from college. Her journey was fueled by a deep belief that faith, hard work, and perseverance could overcome any obstacle.

My dad, one of 13 children, shared a similar story. He was an athlete, playing baseball and basketball in high school and later earning a scholarship to Central College in McPherson, Kansas. Although his sports career was cut short by injury, he never lost faith in the importance of hard work and determination. His pride in his accomplishments, whether on the baseball field or in the buildings he helped construct, was evident in everything he did.

EARLY TESTING OF FAITH: LOUISIANA FLO-JO

Faith was the foundation of my childhood, and it was tested early. I idolized Florence Griffith Joyner, better known as Flo-Jo, the track star who captivated the world during the 1984 Summer Olympics.

She was everything I felt a woman should be: beautiful, with long flowing hair, and a track star. I wanted to be a track star just like her—fast, strong, and unbeatable.

In the fifth grade, during our school's field day, I was confident that

I could win the 100-yard dash. I had beaten everyone in my class to earn the right to represent my class in the race. In my mind, I was already the next Flo-Jo.

However, the day before the official field day, we practiced against other classes, and my Flo-Jo dreams came crashing to a halt when I lost to a girl from another class.

I felt defeated. Flo-Jo didn't lose, and neither did Kiki. I was not a loser. Later that night, I prayed as hard as a fifth grader could and asked God to give me the speed of Flo-Jo so I could beat that little speedster the next day.

The next day, in my mind, it was game on. All day, I was ready and anxious, but I knew I had prayed to win, and God was going to help me. Plus, I couldn't let my "shero" Flo-Jo down. My faith was strong, and I believed with all my heart that God would help me.

The day seemed to drag on forever, with all the other activities going on. Other kids were enjoying all the games. There was kickball, wheelbarrow races, and a bunch of other games. In my mind, they were a sheer waste of time. Racing was all that mattered. I knew the 100-yard dash was at the end of the day, and that was where my attention was.

I remember her racing style from the day before—she ran vertically and swung her arms wildly. Her arms were actually moving faster than her legs, which made her seem even faster.

Finally, the moment arrived.

"On your mark, get set, go!"

We were off.

Her arms were swinging, and I was zeroed in on the cones beside the finish line. The entire fifth grade was lined up on either side of the end of the racing lanes.

"Go Kiki!!" I could hear the kids cheering faintly, but I was as focused as I thought Flo-Jo would be. As we ran for what seemed like an eternity, I could see the wild swinging arms in my peripheral vision. Then, they faded out of sight as I crossed the finish line.

The kids screamed and cheered my name.

I won! I was out of breath, but the kids rushed me and picked me up. I closed my eyes. My prayers had been answered, and I was officially Flo-Jo… the fifth-grade version.

This early experience taught me that faith isn't just about hoping for the best—it's about believing so deeply in something that you're willing to put in the work, take the risks, and trust that you will succeed, even when the outcome is uncertain.

EARLY TESTING OF FAITH: CHEERING

As I grew older, my faith continued to be tested and strengthened. I became passionate about cheerleading and basketball, driven by a desire to be accepted and to find my place. I spent years preparing for cheerleading tryouts, attending summer camps, and practicing tirelessly.

I thought cheerleading was the path in life for me because I absolutely loved cheering for other people. When we attended sporting events, I would spend my time watching the cheerleaders.

My Grandy's house was located not too far from Webster Junior High School. When there were football games, she and I would walk across the neighbor's yard to the wire fence that separated the residential property from the school property and watch the games. Little did she know that I was watching the cheerleaders and dreaming of the day that I would finally get to wear that uniform and cheer the teams on to victory. In order for my dream to come true, I knew that I needed to be prepared. So, when Mom signed me up for the summer cheerleading camp, I was thrilled.

I remember the anticipation I felt every morning waiting for my pretend big sisters, Oreata and Adundra, to pick me up. Oreata and Adundra were on the high school cheerleading squad. I had an outfit for every day. Since the school colors were red and white, I felt that I needed to dress the part. My hair was pulled neatly back into a ponytail, and I always wore a pretty bow (red or white) because cheerleaders wear bows. I wore a combination of red shorts and a white shirt or vice versa, with matching socks and white shoes because cheerleaders always wore white shoes. My mom did not have to wake me up to get ready because I was motivated. The camp was from 8 a.m. to noon every day for a week. I took camp very seriously. I always tried to line up in front so that I could see and hear clearly. This was to make sure that I was learning the skills that I needed.

Being a cheerleader requires you to have extremely positive, infectious energy, and I had that. What I didn't have yet was the skill and an understanding of the role of a cheerleader. As a cheerleader, you always had to believe (have faith) that your team could win, and you needed a powerful and loud voice to get the attention of the crowd you were trying to lead. A cheerleader also had to be in tune with what was going on during the game. A skilled cheerleader knew just the right cheer or chant to encourage the team to keep fighting for victory. Sometimes fans could get distracted by other things happening during the game, but a skilled cheerleader could reengage the fans to join them in cheering the team to victory. I knew that I was made to do this, and all I needed now was the knowledge and skills. If I could master these things, I would become a better cheerleader, and hopefully, when I got to seventh grade, I'd be ready to try out for the varsity squad.

During those four years of camp, I won the "Most Spirited" award in my age group. My last summer attending the camp was the summer of 1986, as I would be entering sixth grade in the fall and would be eligible to try out for the Webster Junior High School cheerleading squad.

The past four summers attending summer camp had been amazing. I knew that I was prepared and would achieve my dream of becoming a real cheerleader.

Sixth grade marked a huge transition for me. I was now moving to a new school. Transitioning to middle school came with its challenges. First, I had spent the last three years of elementary school in Shreveport, so I didn't know many people. I knew the kids who attended my church and a few who I played biddy ball with, but that was it. As a result, I struggled with making friends and trying to figure out where I belonged. I did have one good friend, though: Ericka Gilbert.

Ericka and I had known each other since we were babies. Our mothers were sorority sisters, and they both attended Mt. Calm Missionary Baptist Church, where they both served as musicians. As kids, Ericka and I sang in the angel choir, and we also played in the biddy ball league together. Ericka's dad, Elliott Gilbert, was the Webster Junior High School basketball coach. We called him Coach Gilbert. As the middle school year was dwindling down, our teachers began to share information during homeroom about transitioning to Webster Junior High School for seventh and eighth grades. I was delighted when they announced cheerleading tryouts. Finally, I was going to get my shot. I wrote down the dates and times. I couldn't wait to get home to tell Mom about it. I remember the school bell ringing and rushing to the cafeteria to tell Grandy that the day had finally come.

When the day of the tryouts arrived, I was nervous but prepared. There were so many emotions I felt: nervous, afraid. Thoughts of self-doubt even entered my mind. I immediately rejected them by reminding myself that I had won the "Most Spirited Camper" award four years in a row, so I was totally prepared to audition.

The cheerleading auditions were held at the Webster Junior High School gymnasium. We attended a three-day clinic where they taught us cheers and chants that we could use for our audition. I swear it looked like every girl in middle school was trying out for the squad. There were at least 60 girls who attended the clinic—60 girls competing for 12 spots. I quickly realized that to have a shot at securing a spot on the team, there was no room for error. I attended the clinic and selected my tryout cheer. I practiced, practiced, practiced. Even at school during recess, I practiced. I didn't sleep well leading up to the audition. However, I knew that if I projected my voice loudly, executed my jumps perfectly and exuded energy and spirit, I would be selected.

Audition day had arrived. Like I did when I attended the summer cheerleading camp, I dressed for success. Wearing Webster's school colors, I showed up with a white t-shirt, navy blue shorts, white socks, and white tennis shoes. I wore my hair in a ponytail and attached a white/navy hair bow to finish off the look. I made sure to put Vaseline on my face, legs, and arms so that I was glistening and sparkling. As participants arrived, we were each given a number. We lined up in numerical order outside the gym and waited for our turn. My stomach was in knots. I was extremely nervous, but I felt ready. I was prepared.

I had trained for this moment. All I had to do was remember what I learned from camp: project my voice loudly, make sure my arm motions were sharp and crisp, point my toes when doing my jumps, and exhibit high energy and spirit. I knew that if I executed, I would be selected.

It was my turn. I ran into the gym, did a cartwheel, jumped in the air, did a toe touch (one of the most difficult jumps), and gave them all the energy that I could. I stood still, pulled my feet together, placed my hands by my side, and put my head down. I took a deep breath, said a quick prayer, then I began.

I lifted my head up with a big smile and said, "Ready (clap), ok (clap)."

Together we will fight,
And together, we will win.
The WJH Wolves
Will win once again.

I did it. I had completed my audition. I was relieved. I was so proud of myself. I did the work, I looked the part, I was prepared, and I executed flawlessly. Now all I had to do was hope that the judges would vote in my favor.

After the auditions were complete, we were all brought back into the gymnasium to learn our fate. The judges completed their deliberations and were ready to announce the 12 people who would make up the seventh-grade cheerleading squad. I listened intently for my number. Six spots had already been secured. There were six spots left, and my number had not been called yet. My stomach was in knots, and my nerves were on edge. I just knew I had done a good enough job to make the team. After what seemed to be forever, I secured the ninth spot on the team. I was ecstatic. I jumped up from the bleachers and ran to the floor—screaming with exhilaration and jumping up and down with the other girls who had been selected. All those days of watching the WJH cheerleaders from the fence behind my grandmother's backyard had finally come to fruition.

It didn't necessarily bring me all the friends that I thought it would, though. The next week at school, there were girls who didn't speak to me anymore. I was really confused. This was one of my first moments in life when I noticed that achieving success doesn't always mean that everyone is happy for you. It was one of the most painful lessons I had to learn, but it was a necessary one. I was a dreamer, and if I was going to achieve my dreams, then I needed to learn early that the journey is a lonely one and acceptance by others is often not a part of the success equation.

I didn't let that deter me.

EARLY TESTING OF FAITH: BASKETBALL

I threw myself into basketball, despite having little experience. During the '80s, you didn't see an emphasis on girls and women playing basketball. Minden was about 30 miles west of Ruston, Louisiana, "Home of the Lady Techsters" of Louisiana Tech University. Teresa Weatherspoon and Venus Lacey were two prominent players who were well-known in the area at that time. The funny thing about all of this is that I never aspired to play basketball.

My friend Ericka loved basketball. Her dad was the coach, and as we were talking at school one day, she asked if I had planned to try out for the team. I hadn't really thought about it. I figured if she was going and all the other girls were going, then I would go. The problem was I hadn't asked my parents for permission to try out. Webster was basically in my Grandy's backyard, so I felt like it wouldn't be that big of a deal if I attended the tryout. I told Grandy my plans and took the bus to WJH for tryouts. Grandy would pick me up later after she got off, and if not, I could walk to her house and wait for her.

This was probably the first of a string of decisions I made without asking permission but seeking forgiveness later. I don't remember much about the tryout except for the fact that I was awful. I had no earthly idea what I was doing. I don't even remember being nervous. Maybe it was because I had no expectations of being selected, especially since I wasn't very good. Luckily, everyone made the team. Coach Gilbert believed if you could run and jump, he could turn you into a player. He believed that he could teach the game to anyone who was willing to listen and do as they were instructed. His faith in me, combined with my willingness to learn and work hard, set me on a path that I hadn't anticipated but was ready to embrace.

Once I learned the basics, I started playing with my brother and the neighbors outside. So at practice, I played with the girls, and at home, I played with the boys. One day, Daddy nailed a rickety, warped bicycle rim to the tree, and that was the basketball rim. That's where I perfected my shot. The ball barely fit through the rim, so if you could get the ball in there, the regular goal was like throwing a rock in the ocean.

In eighth grade, I tried out for the high school basketball team and was given the number 22—my coach's way of passing the torch from a former star player to me. She said, "You have big shoes to fill." She was intentional about giving me that number. It was a moment of validation and an affirmation of my faith in my abilities.

EARLY TESTING OF FAITH: TRACK

My senior year in high school was the culmination of years of hard work and faith. We had worked our way up to being a top team in basketball, finishing as state runners-up the previous two years. As a member of both the cross-country and track-and-field teams, we had qualified to participate in the state track meet all four years, but we had yet to win a state championship.

With senior year coming to an end, we had one chance remaining to secure a state title. As part of the track team, I qualified for state in the 4x200m relay, 4x400m relay, triple jump, and high jump.

One of my favorite events was the 4x200m relay. In track and field, the 4x200m relay was the first running event of the meet, and we had qualified with one of the three fastest times in the state. We had a great opportunity to finally achieve our goal of becoming state champions. I was the anchor of that team. This means that you are most likely the fastest person on your team and that you can lead your team to success. I had also been selected as a captain. We had worked hard to finally put ourselves in a position to win a state championship.

The 4x200m relay is a sprint, and it requires a technique called the blind exchange, where the baton is passed between runners without looking. It's a process that demands faith, trust, and precision. You can't see the baton, but you have to believe that it will be there when you reach for it. This is where faith becomes not just a standalone concept; it's part of a larger framework that guides successful leadership and life. I call this the Blind Exchange Framework, and it's built on three key elements: Faith, Focus, and Forward Momentum. These elements are interconnected, each one building on the other, and together, they form the foundation for blazing your own trail.

THE BLIND EXCHANGE FRAMEWORK (THREE ELEMENTS)

#1 - FAITH

- **Defining Faith**

There are times when you may receive some type of vision or dream of what you believe is possible. That belief in what you've seen in your mind, even though it's not present visually, is the foundation that sets you up for pursuing this goal or idea of what you want to achieve or receive. Faith is the first and most critical element. It's the starting point, the belief that propels you forward even when you can't see the entire path. In the relay race of life, faith is what enables you to reach back for the baton, trusting that it will be there when you need it.

Faith is often defined as complete trust or confidence in someone or something, but it's more than just a passive belief. Faith is an active force that propels you forward, even when the path ahead is unclear. It's the assurance of things hoped for, the conviction of things not seen. Faith is what allows you to move with confidence in the face of uncertainty, believing that there is something greater guiding you, even when you can't see it with your own eyes.

Faith is critical because it provides the foundation for all your actions. It's the reason you take that first step, even when you're uncertain of where the path will lead. It's the anchor that keeps you grounded when everything else seems chaotic. Without faith, it's easy to become paralyzed by doubt, fear, and indecision. Faith gives you the courage to pursue your dreams, to step into the unknown, and to trust that everything will work out as it should.

But faith is not just about believing in something external. It's also about believing in yourself—in your abilities, your instincts, your dreams, and your decisions. There are moments when you envision what you dream is achievable. That dream, although not yet manifested, plants the seed of what's possible. Self-faith is what enables you to take risks, to push beyond your comfort zone, and to persist toward your dream. It's about trusting that you have what it takes to navigate whatever challenges come your way.

- **Developing Faith**

Two elements essential to developing your faith are the ability to listen and the ability to trust your intuition.

1. Listen: In a blind exchange, you rely on verbal cues from your teammate because you're not able to turn around and see the carrier bringing you the baton. The runner has to listen intently for the teammate's signal in order to initiate the baton exchange. Having smooth transitions increases the odds of the team succeeding. Listening, in this context, means being attuned not only to external voices but also to the internal voice that guides you. This could be the voice of a higher power, your own inner wisdom, or the quiet nudges that push you in the right direction.

Listening is more than just hearing; it's about understanding and interpreting the messages that come your way. It's about filtering out the noise and focusing on what truly matters. In life, as in a relay race, there are countless distractions—people offering unsolicited advice, circumstances that test your resolve, and doubts that creep in when you least expect them. But when you listen with intent, you can discern the signals that guide you toward your goals. On our relay team, blocking out the crowd noise and listening intently for the keyword was key to activating a smooth transition for the blind exchange that would enable our team to move forward.

2. Trust your intuition: Intuition is closely linked to faith. Intuition is that inner knowing, the gut feeling that tells you when something is right or wrong. It's often subtle, but it's powerful. When you trust your intuition, you're essentially placing your faith in something beyond logical reasoning. This trust allows you to make decisions that align with your true self, even when they don't make immediate sense to others.

Your intuition is like an internal compass, always pointing you in the direction that's right for you. It's the quiet voice that says, "Take this opportunity," or "Walk away from this situation." Trusting your intuition means having the confidence to follow these prompts, even when the path ahead is unclear. It's about believing that your inner wisdom will guide you to where you need to be.

But what happens when you don't have faith? Without faith, you're likely to be overwhelmed by doubt and fear. You might second-guess your decisions, miss opportunities, or remain stuck in situations that don't serve you. The absence of faith can lead to inaction, preventing you from moving forward and realizing your potential. Without faith, the voice of intuition becomes drowned out by the noise of uncertainty, making it difficult to discern the right path.

#2 - FOCUS

The second element of the Blind Exchange Framework is Focus—the theme of Chapter 2. Focus is about zeroing in on your goals and shutting out distractions. It's the ability to stay committed to your path no matter what obstacles arise. Just like a relay race, where you must focus on your lane and the finish line, focus in life requires discipline and clarity of purpose.

#3 - FORWARD MOMENTUM

The third element of the Blind Exchange Framework is Forward Momentum—the theme of Chapter 3. Forward is the action you take after faith and focus have aligned. It's the momentum that carries you through challenges and towards your goals. In the relay, forward is the sprint to the finish line, the culmination of all the preparation, faith, and focus that came before.

CONCLUSION

As noted previously, in a sprint relay race, the baton is passed through a blind exchange—a process that requires complete trust and precise timing. The runner receiving the baton can't see it coming; they must rely on faith, focus on the race, and move forward with confidence.

As the anchor of my relay team, I knew that my role was crucial. I had to have faith that my teammate would pass the baton smoothly, focus on my part of the race, and then move forward with all the speed and strength I had. This story is not just about a race—it's a metaphor for life and leadership. It demonstrates how faith, focus, and forward momentum are essential to achieving success.

Faith, as the first element of the Blind Exchange Framework, sets the foundation for everything that follows. It's the belief in yourself, your team, and the process. Without faith, there can be no forward momentum. But with it, you can blaze a trail that others will follow.

Faith has been my constant companion, guiding me through every challenge, every decision, every step of the journey. It is the unseen hand that steadies you when the path is unclear, the quiet voice that encourages you to keep going even when the finish line seems distant. As you set out to blaze your own trail, remember that faith is not just a belief—it's the foundation. Trust in it, listen to it, practice it, and let it guide you to places you never imagined you could go.

2
FOCUS

Let's dive deeper into the second pillar of the Blind Exchange Framework—*Focus*. It's essential for transforming faith into action. While faith gives you the belief to start the journey, focus keeps you on the path, ensuring that every step you take is aligned with your ultimate goal. In leadership, focus is what enables you to maintain momentum, guide your team effectively, and navigate the challenges that inevitably arise along the way.

THE RACE BEGINS

The day had finally arrived. It was time to compete in the state championship, the culmination of years of hard work, training, and faith. As we began to line up, I was full of emotions. I could feel a mixture of excitement and nerves coursing through my body. My heart was pounding, my hands were shaking, and my breathing was rapid. It was time to compete. There were so many things happening. I was very nervous, but I was super excited to finally have the chance to get on the track and prove that we belonged, that it was our time, and that this year would be our year to finally finish as state champions.

Teams were warming up and beginning to line up on the track. As we prepared to start the race, I couldn't help but glance to my left and right, sizing up the competition. The other teams looked formidable, their warm-up routines sharp and precise. Watching them, I began to feel a pang of doubt. Were we really ready? Could we keep up with these teams that seemed so well-prepared? The more I watched, the more I started to question our process—the method that had gotten us this far.

Most teams follow the blind exchange method because it's a sprint. In track, lanes four, five, and six are usually the fastest lanes, and we were in one of those lanes—a testament to our hard work and skill. But as I watched the other teams, their confidence and precision began to shake my own. I started to wonder if maybe their process was better than ours. Maybe, just maybe, if I adjusted our approach, we could match their speed and precision.

But then, the official called us to the line. "On your mark," he said, and we all got into position. My mind was racing, but I tried to push the doubts aside. "Get set," he commanded, and we all stilled, waiting for the signal. The shot from the starting pistol echoed through the air, and we were off.

THE EXCHANGE

The first exchange went smoothly. Our team was in the top three, just as we had hoped. The second exchange was equally successful. My teammates were doing an incredible job, and now it was my turn. I was the third exchange, the anchor who would bring it home.

As my teammate approached me for the third and final exchange, I could feel the pressure mounting. She hit the mark, and I took off, accelerating as fast as I could while staying within the exchange zone. I was ready to hear the keyword—"smoke"—that would signal me to reach back for the baton.

But then, something strange happened. In a moment of doubt, I made a split-second decision that would change everything. Instead of sticking to our process—the blind exchange—I turned around to receive the baton. I thought that by seeing it, I could ensure a smoother exchange. But the opposite happened.

I dropped the baton.

In that instant, everything changed. As the baton slipped from my hand, I decelerated, losing the momentum we had built. My body was now out of position, and the race that we had worked so hard for was slipping away. The dropped baton wasn't just a physical error; it was a signal that we would not finish in the top three. We would finish last.

LEADERSHIP LESSONS: THE IMPACT OF FOCUS

That moment taught me a powerful lesson about the importance of focus. When I turned around to look back, I lost focus of the finish line. I lost sight of our goal and the process that had been designed to get us there. In leadership, losing focus can have similar consequences. It can cause you to lose momentum, get out of position, and ultimately fail to achieve your goals.

In that race, my decision to abandon our process and try something different was a violation of the trust that my teammates had placed in me. They had trusted me to lead them, to stick to our plan, and to execute it flawlessly. But when I lost focus, I let them down.

Focus is about more than just keeping your eyes on the prize. It's about maintaining trust, staying committed to your process, and resisting the temptation to deviate when things get tough. In leadership, focus means making sure that every action you take and every decision you make are aligned with the goals you've set for yourself and your team.

When you lose focus, you lose momentum. And when you lose momentum, it becomes harder to move forward. Just as I decelerated when I dropped the baton, losing focus in leadership can cause you to slow down, lose your way, and ultimately fail to reach your destination.

FOCUS AND BLAZING YOUR OWN TRAIL

Focus is the compass that guides you when blazing your own trail. It's what allows you to carve out a unique path in a world full of distractions, competing interests, and external pressures. When you have a clear focus, you're not just moving forward blindly; you're moving with purpose, clarity, and direction. This intentionality is what sets trailblazers apart from those who merely follow in the footsteps of others.

MULTIPLE PATHS TO SUCCESS: TRUSTING YOUR OWN PROCESS

When you are blazing your own trail, it's important to remember that there are multiple ways to achieve the same goal. In the world of leadership, there isn't just one "right" way to succeed. Each team and each leader has their own unique process that aligns with their strengths, values, and goals. What works for one person or one team may not work for another, and that's okay. The temptation to look at others' success and think that their way might be better is strong, especially in moments of doubt or pressure. But when you focus too much on what others are doing, you risk losing sight of your own process—what has been working for you all along. The key is to stay committed to your process, trust the foundation you've built, and focus on refining and perfecting your approach.

During the relay race, I let myself be distracted by how well the other teams were performing. I started to doubt our method, even though it had gotten us to the state finals. In trying to adopt their approach, I lost focus on our strengths and what made our team successful. This not only cost us the race but also taught me that true success comes from trusting in your own process, not from trying to replicate someone else's.

Focus on your process, and don't be swayed by the noise around you. I'll tell you this: five plus four is nine, and so is six plus three, one plus eight, two plus seven, and zero plus nine. There are countless ways to reach the same destination, but the path that is right for you is the one that aligns with your strengths, your team's abilities, and your shared vision. When you stay focused on your process, you're not just following a path—you're creating one that is uniquely yours.

LOSING FOCUS AND ITS IMPACT ON ALIGNMENT WITH YOUR VISION

Losing focus doesn't just slow you down; it can also pull you out of alignment with your vision. Your vision is your guiding star—the overarching goal that all your actions should lead towards. When you are focused, every decision and every step you take aligns with that vision, moving you closer to your ultimate goal. However, when you lose focus, you risk veering off course and making decisions that don't serve your long-term objectives.

In the relay race, the moment I decided to look back and deviate from our established process, I broke alignment with our team's vision of winning the state championship. That split-second decision wasn't just about a dropped baton; it was about losing sight of the bigger picture. My actions, driven by doubt and distraction, no longer supported our goal. Instead, they derailed us, pushing us further away from our intended outcome.

In leadership, maintaining alignment with your vision is critical. Your vision is what keeps you and your team grounded, providing a clear direction for all your efforts. When you lose focus, it's easy to make choices that seem beneficial in the short term but ultimately pull you away from your long-term goals. This misalignment can lead to confusion within your team, a loss of trust, and a dilution of your efforts.

To stay aligned with your vision, it's essential to continuously bring your focus back to your core goals. Regularly reassess your actions and decisions, ensuring they are in harmony with the bigger picture. This alignment requires discipline and a constant reminder of why you started in the first place. When your focus is aligned with your vision, every step you take propels you closer to achieving your goals.

THE POWER OF FOCUS IN OVERCOMING OBSTACLES

Every trailblazer encounters obstacles—moments when the path forward seems unclear or when the challenges ahead feel insurmountable. In these moments, focus becomes your greatest ally. It's what enables you to maintain momentum even when the going gets tough. When you're focused, you can see beyond the immediate challenges to the bigger picture. You can stay committed to your goals, knowing that the obstacles are just temporary hurdles on the way to success.

In the relay race, losing focus led to a loss of momentum, which in turn led to failure. Similarly, in life, when you lose focus, you risk stalling your progress. You might become bogged down by challenges or distracted by setbacks, losing sight of the end goal. But with focus, you can navigate these obstacles with resilience and determination, keeping your eyes fixed on the finish line.

Focus also helps you make strategic decisions in the face of adversity. When you're clear about your goals, you can assess challenges more effectively, determining the best course of action to overcome them. This strategic clarity is what enables trailblazers to push through difficult times and emerge stronger on the other side.

FOCUS AND AUTHENTICITY

Blazing your own trail requires authenticity—being true to yourself and your unique vision. Focus is the tool that keeps you aligned with this authenticity. In a world where it's easy to be influenced by others' successes, focus helps you resist the temptation to follow trends that don't align with your values or goals. It keeps you grounded in your own purpose, ensuring that the path you're creating is truly your own.

During the relay race, my decision to mimic the other teams was a departure from our authentic process. I let the pressure of competition and the fear of failure push me away from what had been working for us. This was a critical mistake, one that highlighted the importance of staying true to your own methods, even when others around you are doing things differently.

In leadership and in life, authenticity is key to blazing your own trail. When you remain focused on your own vision, you can make decisions that are aligned with your true self, rather than being swayed by external influences. This authenticity is what gives your path its unique value, setting you apart as a true trailblazer.

FOCUS AS A CONTINUOUS PRACTICE

Focus is not a one-time effort; it's a continuous practice. It's something you must cultivate and maintain throughout your journey. Blazing your own trail requires consistent focus, as distractions and challenges will always arise. It's about staying disciplined, keeping your eyes on the finish line, and regularly realigning yourself with your goals.

In practice, this means setting aside time to reflect on your progress, reassessing your goals, and making adjustments as needed. It means being mindful of the distractions that can pull you off course and developing strategies to minimize their impact. It also means staying connected to your purpose, using it as a touchstone to guide your decisions and actions.

Focus is like the lens through which you view your journey. When the lens is clear and sharp, you can see the path ahead with clarity and make decisions that are in line with your goals. But when the lens is blurred by distractions, doubts, or external pressures, the path becomes harder to navigate. This is why continuous focus is so critical —it keeps your vision clear and your actions purposeful.

THE CONSEQUENCES OF LOSING FOCUS

As we saw in the relay race, losing focus can have significant consequences. Just think: when I turned back, my body was now out of alignment, and my focus was no longer on the finish line. If the goal is to get to the finish line, why would I be looking back in the opposite direction? Have you ever tried to walk one way and look another? You probably can't walk a straight line if you've ever tried to do that. As a matter of fact, why don't you try to do it right now? Get up. I want you to try to walk forward while looking backward, but be careful.

Losing focus causes you to lose momentum, make poor decisions, and ultimately fail to achieve your goals. When you lose focus, you risk straying from your path, getting caught up in distractions, and missing out on opportunities that could have propelled you forward.

In the context of leadership, losing focus can lead to a breakdown in trust. Your team relies on you to stay committed to the shared vision and to guide them toward success. When you lose focus, you not only jeopardize your own goals but also the goals of those who depend on you. This can erode trust, undermine morale, and weaken the overall effectiveness of your team.

Perhaps the greatest consequence of losing focus is that it can prevent you from fully realizing your potential. Blazing your own trail requires you to be fully present, fully committed, and fully focused on the path you're creating. When you lose focus, you dilute your efforts, spreading yourself too thin and diminishing the impact you can have. To blaze your own trail successfully, you must remain steadfast in your focus, ensuring that every step you take is purposeful and aligned with your ultimate vision.

CONCLUSION: FOCUS AS A GUIDING FORCE

Focus is the guiding force that enables you to blaze your own trail with confidence and clarity. It's what keeps you aligned with your unique vision, helps you navigate obstacles, and ensures that every action you take is intentional and purposeful. In the Blind Exchange Framework, *focus* is the crucial link between *faith* and *forward momentum*. Without focus, even the strongest faith can falter, and even the best intentions can go unrealized.

But what happens when, despite your best efforts, things don't work out the way you want them to? What do you do when you lose focus or when a setback derails your progress? This is where the true test of leadership and perseverance begins. For me, after dropping the baton and losing the race, I still had three more events to compete in that day. This meant I had three more chances to achieve my goal of becoming a state champion.

The lesson here is that focus alone is not enough—you must also know how to move forward after a setback. How do you pick yourself up, regain your momentum, and continue pursuing your goals? The answer lies in the third element of the Blind Exchange Framework: Forward Momentum.

In Chapter 3, we will explore how to harness forward momentum toward your goals and how to push past failures, even when the path becomes challenging. Forward momentum embodies resilience, determination, and the unwavering belief that your next step can still lead to success, regardless of what happened before.

3
FORWARD MOMENTUM

Chapter 2 ended with the drop of the baton and losing focus, and you know, it was a terrible moment. It really sucks when we make those mistakes. But how we respond to those mistakes is really critical, and Chapter 3 helps us get there.

MOVING FORWARD: THE TRIPLE-A METHOD

1. Assess
The first step in the Triple-A method is to assess the situation. This step is foundational to moving forward after a setback. It requires taking a deliberate pause to carefully analyze what went wrong and why it happened. When I dropped the baton during the relay, it wasn't just about a physical mistake; it was the culmination of mental missteps that began when I allowed myself to be distracted by the other competitors. I had let doubt creep in, and this ultimately led to a momentary lapse in judgment where I strayed from our team's well-practiced process. This kind of assessment isn't just about recognizing the mistake—it's about understanding the deeper, underlying causes that

led to that moment. It's about peeling back the layers of what occurred to truly grasp the factors that contributed to the error.

Assessing the situation also means considering all the contributing factors—both internal, like self-doubt, and external, like the pressure of competition. I had to confront the reality that my focus shifted because I allowed intimidation to influence my decisions. This acknowledgment was crucial because it provided clarity on how my mindset affected my actions. Moreover, assessment isn't just about identifying what went wrong; it's also about recognizing what was right before the mistake occurred. This dual focus helps you understand not only where you faltered but also where your strengths lie. By assessing both the positives and the negatives, you can build a clearer picture of what needs to be maintained and what needs to change.

Another important aspect of assessment is its role in preparing you to move forward with renewed purpose. By thoroughly evaluating the situation, you arm yourself with the knowledge and insights necessary to avoid similar mistakes in the future. This process of reflection is critical in blazing your own trail because it ensures that each step forward is informed by past experiences. It's about learning from the past to shape a better future. Assessment gives you the clarity needed to make adjustments and reinforces your commitment to your path. Without this critical evaluation, you risk repeating the same mistakes, which can derail your progress and hinder your ability to lead effectively. Considering I still had three more events to compete in that day, I needed to get it together.

2. Acknowledge
Once you've assessed the situation, the next vital step is to acknowledge the error, both to yourself and to those affected. Acknowledgment is more than just admitting that a mistake was made; it's about taking full responsibility for the consequences of that mistake. As the leader of my relay team, I had to

confront the reality that my decision to deviate from our process led to the dropped baton. This wasn't an easy admission, but it was necessary. I had to face my teammates, look them in the eye, and say, "This was my fault, and I apologize." This act of acknowledgment was crucial for rebuilding the trust that had been shaken by my error. It's not just about admitting fault; it's about owning the impact of that fault on the team and on our shared goals.

Taking ownership of a mistake is not a sign of weakness; it's a demonstration of strength and integrity. In leadership, the ability to acknowledge errors openly and sincerely is what differentiates effective leaders from those who deflect blame. When you own your mistakes, you show your team that you are accountable, not just for successes but also for failures. This fosters an environment of trust and transparency, where team members feel safe to admit their own mistakes and learn from them. Acknowledging the error also sets the stage for constructive dialogue about how to move forward, turning a negative experience into a valuable learning opportunity. It's about creating a culture where mistakes are seen as part of the learning process, rather than something to be feared or avoided.

Acknowledgment also involves understanding the emotional impact of the mistake on yourself and your team. It's important to validate the feelings of disappointment, frustration, or even anger that might arise. By doing so, you help your team process the event and begin the healing process. This step is critical because it allows everyone involved to come to terms with what happened, making it possible to move forward together. Acknowledgment is not just about saying, "I'm sorry"; it's about showing empathy, understanding the repercussions of the mistake, and committing to do better. This kind of leadership strengthens the bonds within the team and lays a strong foundation for future challenges. When you acknowledge a mistake, you pave the way for rebuilding trust and restoring confidence, both in yourself and in those you lead.

3. Adjust
The final step in the Triple-A Method is to adjust your alignment, which means making the necessary changes to ensure that you are back on track toward your goals. After assessing the situation and acknowledging the mistake, it's time to take actionable steps to correct your course. For me, this meant reaffirming our process and committing to blocking out distractions. I had to remind myself and my team that the methods we had practiced and perfected were our best path to success. Adjusting my alignment wasn't just about making corrections; it was about strengthening our approach and ensuring that we were better prepared for the remaining events. Adjustment is about more than just fixing what went wrong—it's about evolving your strategy to be more resilient and effective moving forward.

Adjustment requires a proactive mindset. It's about not only correcting the specific error but also refining your overall strategy to enhance future performance. In the context of my relay team, adjusting meant going back to the fundamentals that had brought us success in the past. I needed to refocus on our process, eliminate any doubts, and trust in the preparation that had gotten us this far. This step was crucial because it involved not just a physical adjustment in how we approached the remaining races but also a mental adjustment in how I approached leadership. I needed to regain the confidence of my team and show them that we could still achieve our goals despite the setback. This adjustment is a vital part of blazing your own trail because it emphasizes the importance of resilience and adaptability in the face of challenges.

Adjusting your alignment also involves setting new intentions and making sure that your actions are in sync with your revised strategy. It's about recalibrating your focus and making deliberate changes to avoid repeating the same mistakes. This might mean implementing new practices, refining existing ones, or even changing your mindset altogether. In leadership, this step is critical because it demonstrates resilience and adaptability—qualities that are essential for long-term success. When you effectively adjust your alignment, you're not just recovering from a setback; you're positioning yourself and your team to achieve your goals with renewed focus and determination. Adjusting allows you to take control of your journey, ensuring that each step you take is intentional and aligned with your ultimate vision, helping you blaze your own trail with confidence and purpose.

PICKING UP THE BATON: A SYMBOL OF MOVING FORWARD

When I dropped the baton, I was immediately faced with a critical decision: leave it on the ground and accept defeat, or pick it up and finish the race, no matter the outcome. In that split second, I chose to pick it up and run as fast as I could to the finish line. This decision wasn't just about completing the race; it was a symbolic act of resilience and determination. Picking up the baton represented my refusal to let a mistake define the outcome and my commitment to continue pursuing my goal despite the setback. It was about demonstrating to myself and to others that failure is not the end—it's an opportunity to learn, grow, and keep pushing forward.

The act of picking up the baton goes beyond the physical action; it's a powerful metaphor for leadership and life. In our personal and professional lives, we are all bound to stumble at some point. We may face setbacks, make mistakes, or experience failures that challenge our confidence and resolve. But what truly matters is how we respond to those moments. Will we let them stop us, or will we choose to get back up, realign ourselves with our vision, and keep moving forward? Picking up the baton is about reclaiming control over your journey, acknowledging that while the path may not be perfect, it's still within your power to continue.

Moreover, this decision to move forward is a testament to the strength of your character and the depth of your commitment to your goals. It's easy to become discouraged after a setback, to feel like giving up is the simpler choice. But trailblazers don't choose the easy path—they choose the path that leads to growth, even if it's fraught with challenges. Picking up the baton symbolizes your resilience, your ability to bounce back, and your unwavering dedication to the journey ahead. It's a reminder that no matter how many times you fall, you have the power to rise again and continue on your path, stronger and more determined.

RESET AND GAIN MOMENTUM

After dropping the baton, the race may have been lost, but the day was far from over. I still had three more events to compete in: the high jump, the triple jump, and the 4x400m relay. This presented me with a new challenge—how to mentally reset and prepare for the remaining opportunities to achieve my goal of becoming a state champion. The disappointment of the baton drop was fresh, but I knew that dwelling on it would only hinder my performance in the upcoming events. I had to quickly assess what went wrong, acknowledge my mistake, and adjust my mindset to focus on what was still possible. This process of resetting after a disappointment is crucial in any endeavor because it allows you to shift your energy from the past to the future.

Resetting after a setback is not just about forgetting what happened; it's about learning from it and using that knowledge to fuel your next steps. It requires mental fortitude to not dwell on past mistakes but to refocus on what lies ahead. This ability to reset quickly is a skill that separates those who achieve their goals from those who are paralyzed by failure. You must learn to transition swiftly from disappointment, realign with your goals, and channel your energy into the next opportunity. This is how you gain momentum and continue to progress, even when things don't go as planned. It's about understanding that every challenge is also an opportunity to refine your approach and prove your resilience.

In the context of my remaining events, resetting was about more than just focusing on the next jump or relay. It was about reclaiming my confidence and reinforcing my belief in my abilities. The high jump and triple jump were events where I had strong potential, and the 4x400m relay was another chance to contribute to my team's success. By resetting my mindset, I was able to approach each event with a renewed sense of purpose. I reminded myself of the preparation and practice that had brought me this far, and I committed to giving my best effort in each remaining event. This mental reset was crucial, as it allowed me to put the baton drop behind me and focus on what I could still achieve.

THE IMPORTANCE OF SWIFT ACTION

When moving forward, particularly after a setback, it's essential to act swiftly. In a 4x200m race, there's no time to dwell on mistakes—you have to quickly understand what went wrong, adjust your approach, and keep moving. The same principle applies in leadership and life. The quicker you can assess, acknowledge, and adjust, the faster you can get back in alignment with your goals. Swift action is necessary because the longer you linger on a mistake, the more it can weigh you down, sapping your energy and diverting your focus from what still lies ahead. The key is to transition quickly, learning from the error but not allowing it to define your next steps.

In the high jump and triple jump events that followed, I knew I couldn't afford to repeat the same mistake that led to the baton drop. I had to refocus on my process, blocking out distractions and trusting the preparation that had gotten me this far. By doing so, I was able to perform at my highest level, winning the state championship in the triple jump and setting the school record. This outcome was a direct result of my ability to act swiftly, reset my mindset, and approach each event with a clear focus on success. Swift action doesn't mean rushing through without thought—it means being deliberate and purposeful in how you respond to challenges, ensuring that each step you take moves you closer to your goal.

This experience taught me that dwelling on past errors only prolongs your journey to success. You must learn from your mistakes, adjust your actions, and move forward with renewed focus. The ability to swiftly assess, acknowledge, and adjust is what allows you to maintain momentum and continue progressing, even when faced with setbacks. It's about keeping your eyes on the prize, staying aligned with your vision, and taking decisive action that propels you forward. In leadership and in life, those who can move forward quickly and effectively are the ones who ultimately blaze their own trail and achieve their goals.

THE POWER OF CHOICE

If you're going to be a trailblazer and a leader, it's essential to understand the power of choice. Moving forward is a decision that only you can make. No one else can do it for you—not your parents, not your coach, not your boss. This realization is empowering because it reminds you of the control you have over your own success. Every action you take, every decision you make, contributes to the path you're creating. When faced with setbacks, it's your choice whether to let them define you or to use them as stepping stones to greater achievement. The power of choice is at the heart of resilience and perseverance, two qualities that are essential for anyone looking to blaze their own trail.

The foundational elements we've discussed—faith, focus, and now forward momentum—are all interconnected. Even when you stumble, these principles will help you pick yourself up, reset, and continue toward your goals with determination and clarity. Faith gives you the belief that you can achieve your goals, focus keeps you on track, and forward movement drives you to keep going, no matter what obstacles arise. Understanding the power of choice allows you to harness these principles effectively, ensuring that every step you take is purposeful and aligned with your ultimate vision.

As you continue on your journey, remember that the power to move forward lies within you. The choices you make will determine the trajectory of your path and the impact you leave behind. By embracing the power of choice, you empower yourself to overcome challenges, learn from mistakes, and keep pushing forward. This is what it means to be a trailblazer: not simply following a path but actively creating one that reflects your values, your goals, and your unique vision. It's about taking ownership of your journey, making intentional choices, and moving forward with confidence, knowing that you have the power to shape your own success.

CONCLUSION

If you truly want to be the best version of yourself, if you are determined to blaze your own trail, you must learn to view failures not as roadblocks but as teachable moments. The baton drop at that particular meet was one of the most significant failures I faced, yet it became one of my greatest teachers. Instead of letting it define me, I chose to assess what went wrong, acknowledge my mistake, and adjust my approach. By embracing the Triple A Method within the context of the Blind Exchange Framework—Faith, Focus, and Forward Momentum—I was able to move forward with renewed purpose and determination. This wasn't just about picking up where I left off; it was about elevating myself to a higher level of performance by integrating the core elements of faith in the process, maintaining focus on the goal, and pushing forward despite setbacks.

The Blind Exchange Framework has guided me through this journey, and it can guide you as well. Faith was the foundation that allowed me to believe in the possibility of success, even when circumstances seemed unfavorable. It's the belief in something greater than what you can see—the trust that your efforts will lead to the desired outcome. Focus was what kept me aligned with my goals, ensuring that I didn't lose sight of what mattered most, even amidst distractions. Forward Momentum, the final element, was the driving force that propelled me to act, to keep moving, and to finish what I started. When I dropped the baton, I relied on these elements to regain my footing and continue the race. This approach is not just applicable to that moment on the track; it's a powerful framework for navigating any challenge in life.

Because I was able to move forward using the Triple A Method, those mental and corrective behaviors enabled me to compete at my highest level. The result? I achieved the goal I had set for myself—I became a state champion in the triple jump and set another school record. But more importantly, I proved to myself that the Blind Exchange Framework works. Faith in the process, maintaining focus, and the relentless push forward allowed me to transform a moment of failure into a stepping stone for success. This is what happens when you decide to utilize the Triple A Method within the Blind Exchange Framework and take decisive action. You move forward, you finish, and you finish strong, consistently aligning with your process and goals. It's crucial to remember that in these moments, distractions will always be present, but staying true to your path and moving forward swiftly are the keys to reaching your desired destination.

As I prepared to transition to college, even more challenging scenarios would present themselves. Each one would test my ability to apply the principles of the Blind Exchange Framework to achieve the success I envisioned for myself. But the lessons I learned on that track field stayed with me. Believe in yourself, and don't shy away from the challenges that come your way. Don't be afraid to learn these lessons now—they will shape you into a leader who is prepared to handle whatever comes next. You don't always need someone to tell you what to do; instead, pay attention, listen, and learn from your experiences. These moments of self-reflection and growth will prepare you to lead with excellence.

When I was 17, these were the lessons that began to mold my leadership journey. By the time I was 25, I had become a head coach, a role that demanded every ounce of the resilience, focus, and forward movement I had cultivated. While "The Baton Story" is just one of many experiences that reinforced the foundational elements of blazing my own trail, it stands out as a critical life event that profoundly influenced every decision I made moving forward. It taught me how to respond when things didn't go my way, and it instilled in me the importance of continuous growth within the framework of Faith, Focus, and Forward Momentum.

As you prepare and reflect on your own life experiences, I encourage you to examine them closely through the lens of the Blind Exchange Framework. Every unique experience you have is a potential source of wisdom and leadership lessons that can position you for success in all of your endeavors.

Faith will help you believe in the possibilities even when they are not immediately visible.

Focus will keep you aligned with your goals, ensuring that you don't stray from the path you've set for yourself.

Forward Momentum will give you the energy to keep going, to pick up the baton after every fall, and to continue blazing your own trail. The path you create will be defined not just by your victories, but also by how you rise from setbacks, how you learn from each stumble, and how you keep moving forward with unyielding determination.

PART 2

CHALLENGES OF BLAZING YOUR OWN TRAIL

4

MANAGING TRANSITION

I ended my high school career as a state champion, and I was armed and ready to take my talents to college. I was very excited about going to college. Having the opportunity to play sports in high school and achieve the success we did was amazing.

But I always wondered, *Am I really as good as I believe I am?* When I graduated from high school, I had several academic and athletic scholarship opportunities to attend college. I was a very good basketball player, earning All-State honors and being selected to play for the West side in the state All-Star game.

I remember contemplating whether I wanted to attend college on a basketball scholarship or a track scholarship. At some point, I thought, why do I have to choose? It would be great if I could do both. Unfortunately, I didn't have any scholarship offers that would allow me to participate in both.

As I thought about my decision, I reflected on what I loved most about basketball. It was knowing that people would pay money to buy tickets to come to basketball games. Track wasn't the same. We didn't always get the same fanfare, and we didn't always have a crowded stadium to come and watch us run. Ultimately, I decided that basketball was what I wanted to do because I really loved the roar of the crowd. I loved having people there who could cheer for me. My parents, all my siblings, my grandma, my cousins, everybody would come to the games. They would wear sweatshirts that said, *"Sister of number 22," "Mother of number 22,"* and *"Father of number 22."* It felt really good to have all those people come, witness, and be there to celebrate, cheer, and call my name during games.

I also wanted to attend a school that was close enough for my family to come see me, but far enough away for me to feel like I was on my own. And I wanted to see if I could really make it in the real world. Being from a small country town like Minden, Louisiana, I really wanted the opportunity to see if I could compete with other young women from across the country. After visiting two other colleges, I attended South Plains College (SPC) in Levelland, Texas, which was approximately an eight-hour drive from home. One thing I knew for sure: No one knew me. South Plains didn't have a track team, but I figured that even though they didn't have one, I might pick up track again if I transferred to a school that did after my two years at junior college. I might eventually pursue my goals and maybe go to the Olympics. One of the reasons I chose to attend junior college was because I was considered small for the position I played in high school.

I played a combination of shooting guard and small forward. I felt like I needed a little more physical and athletic development before I could go to a larger Division I school. The lady who recruited me was an amazing coach named Cheryl Watson. I had really developed a great relationship with her. She had come to watch me play in the state championship basketball game and briefly spoke with my parents and me afterward. She was a part of setting up the official visit. I remember being so excited about developing that relationship with her. I felt like she was personally invested in my growth as a player.

When I arrived on campus for orientation, I was introduced to a new assistant coach. I learned that Coach Watson had accepted an assistant coach position at a Division I school. I was disappointed, and I remember feeling concerned about my ability to be successful at the school. Would the new assistant coach be as committed to me? I will say that I kind of felt tricked. I felt alone. Who was going to advocate for me now?

I didn't know the head coach very well either. As a result, the first year triggered a series of tough situations. New coach, new environment, new teammates—everything was new. I was intimidated by all the changes that were happening.

Transition is a fundamental part of life, especially when you're blazing your own trail. Just as in a relay race, where the baton must be passed smoothly from one runner to the next, our personal and professional journeys require us to navigate transitions with precision and confidence. My journey from high school to college represented a significant transition, much like the baton exchanges in the 4x200m relay that I had mastered during my athletic career. In that relay, the successful handoff of the baton was crucial to the team's performance; similarly, moving from one phase of life to another requires careful attention to how we manage the handoff from the familiar to the unknown. The shift from high school to college was more than just a physical move; it was a psychological and emotional transition that required me to reassess my identity as an athlete, a student, and a person.

EMOTIONAL RESPONSES TO TRANSITION

Transitions are not just about the external changes we face—they also provoke deep emotional responses that can either propel us forward or hold us back. One of the interesting challenges I faced during my freshman year in college was the coach examining my size and my ability to determine if playing the shooting guard/small forward position would be the best fit. Based on my particular skill set and size, he believed I should consider switching my position from shooting guard to point guard. I was not happy with this recommended change. I did not do a good job as a point guard, and I was upset because I was not performing well. I was starting to lose my confidence and question whether or not I was cut out to play college basketball.

LOSING CONFIDENCE

Loss of confidence is another powerful emotional response to transition. As I struggled to adapt to the new position my coach assigned me, I began to doubt my abilities. Confidence, which had been one of my greatest assets in high school, started to erode. I was no longer the star player who could rely on familiar skills and strategies; I was in uncharted territory, and the uncertainty of it all made me question whether I was truly capable of succeeding in this new environment. Losing confidence can be a significant barrier in any transition, as it affects your willingness to take risks, embrace new challenges, and trust in your ability to overcome obstacles.

The position was challenging because I had to transition my mindset. The point guard's role is to construct plays that lead to other players scoring. It's a different way of leading that I was honestly uncomfortable with. Setting other people up to score was not in my purview. To be a good point guard, I needed better court vision. And to have better court vision, I needed to be a better ball handler. One of the weakest areas of my game was ball handling. My inability to handle the ball meant that I was looking down at the ball when I was trying to change direction, which was critical to setting up my teammates. And because I was looking down, my vision was limited, which impacted my ability to see and assess what was happening on the court.

I was ineffective in setting up other teammates to score because my vision was impaired by my inability to handle the ball. It was not in alignment with what I wanted. I was more comfortable playing with a very narrow focus on scoring myself, rather than considering the dynamics of the entire team. Because of that, I did not perform well.

My coach provided me with ball-handling drills during practices that would help me regain my confidence and become a better ball-handler. Unfortunately, I rejected most of it.

REJECTING FEEDBACK

I did not like the idea that I needed to shift my position. I felt like I was better at the shooting guard position and that my coach was making a bad decision by trying to transition me to point guard. I felt my success was being sabotaged and that there were allegiances on the team working against me. I had a bad attitude about it. I said things to myself like, *I don't even know why the coach is making me do this. It's not like there's a professional women's basketball league in the United States, anyway.* I saw my participation in sports as a means to an end, and this scholarship would help me get my degree so that I could eventually pursue whatever career I wanted. That's what I was trying to do.

I was not trying to be a professional basketball player. My coach choosing to focus on a position that was not relevant to my end goal seemed like a waste of time. So, the constant battle between my coach and me as he continued to provide me with these opportunities to develop my skills and to challenge me, and me mentally deciding that I just didn't see this for myself, worked against me.

PLAYING THE BLAME GAME

My mom and dad showed up at my first game. My parents drove eight hours just to see me play, and I didn't get any playing time. At the end of that game, my mom asked me, "Why aren't you playing?"

"Because the coach doesn't like me," I replied, then launched into a barrage of complaints and excuses to my parents about my coach and all the decisions he was making that I didn't agree with. I went on and on, accusing him of not giving me a fair shot, putting me in this position to fail, and saying that I didn't think it was fair.

As my mom listened to me vent for approximately two to three minutes, I began to see a change in her disposition. She started to shake her head in disagreement, and I knew that I was in trouble. She eventually held her hand up, which meant for me to be quiet. "No, that's not it," she said, looking me straight in my eyes. "It's not the coach. It's YOU."

I was so upset. Tears started to fall from my eyes because now I felt like my mom was taking the coach's side. It felt like the ultimate betrayal.

"I know what you're capable of," she continued. "If you were doing what you were supposed to be doing, you would be on that court."

It was one of the most profound lessons I could have learned: I had the power to change my situation if I was willing to change my mindset.

How many times have you blamed other people for not achieving your goals? I rejected the instruction my coach was trying to give me. I mentally decided that I did not want to make this shift. And when I got into practice, I did not do my best. I was the person controlling my actions, not my coach. My coach was providing me with the challenges that were needed, but I decided that I did not want to perform at my highest ability. The result was that I did not get playing time. My mother simply helped me connect my mindset to the outcomes I was receiving. My decision to reject instruction (not listen) and not give my best effort (not practice) were directly related to limited playing time. I appreciate that my mother was clear and reassured me that I was capable of getting it done. I just had to decide to take the necessary action (Triple-A) to get it done. One of the things that's really critical as you continue to grow is that you have to learn that there are people in your life who want to help you and are going to tell you things that you do not want to hear. I was lucky to have a family that did not hold me back and supported me.

BLIND SPOTS

One of the most dangerous aspects of any transition is the presence of blind spots—those areas of our lives or behaviors that we cannot see but can significantly impact our success. Blind spots are particularly challenging because, by their very nature, they are hidden from our view. It often takes someone else to point them out to us, and even then, it can be difficult to acknowledge and address them. In my transition from high school to college, my blind spots included my resistance to change, my refusal to embrace the role of point guard, and the loss of confidence that accompanied these struggles. I didn't realize how these attitudes were holding me back until my mother, serving as my compass and guide, pointed them out to me.

Not everyone's so lucky. I had someone who said to me that I needed to be accountable for the decisions that I was making. She also told me that if I changed my behavior, my outcome would change positively in my favor. Who are the people in your life who tell you the things that you don't want to hear? One of the things I've found in blazing your own trail is that we can sometimes reject sound support. Listening, as I mentioned in Chapter 1, is a critical, foundational element of blazing your own trail. You have to listen to the things you want to hear as well as those you don't want to hear. In this particular instance, my mother was right in rejecting my excuses and attempting to place blame on my coach. I appreciate her admonishing me to look inward.

Given that she was a strategic advisor, someone who cared about me and wanted to see me have the success that she believed I was capable of, I knew that I needed to change my mindset and behavior.

WHO ARE YOUR ADVISORS?

This is the kind of support that sometimes you don't know you need in your life. You need to understand who the critical people are in your life who will tell you the things you don't want to hear. The things you don't want to hear sometimes are the things that you need to hear to help you level up in your leadership and toward achieving your goals. If you just want someone to agree with you and pat you on the back, you will not achieve your highest levels of success.

As I have shared, listening, being able to cut through the noise, and understanding those who are critical to helping you succeed are critical elements of being a trailblazer and leader. You need to have the intuition to know what to receive and what to reject. I had a strong relationship with my mom, who was one of my trusted advisors and someone I knew wanted the best for me. Her support helped me correct my attitude and adjust my actions, enabling me to become a solid, productive member of this new team—someone who could be counted on to contribute to our success.

Throughout my journey, I have had advisors who have been straightforward and honest with me. They told me the truth without worrying about my feelings because their primary concern was helping me become the best version of myself. You need someone in your life who will tell you the truth, whether you want to hear it or not. These people serve as valuable advisors in your journey. Think about having a map or a compass to redirect you if you're going off the path. Since you are blazing your own trail, only *you* can decide the next steps; however, advisors can encourage you and help you reset. You miss out on opportunities to grow when you reject sound wisdom from your advisors. It was clear that, with the attitude and actions that I was taking at that time, I was headed in the wrong direction. This was because I could not see. That's why listening is such a crucial part of the trailblazer journey.

But I was humble enough to receive and listen to what my mom had to say. One of the critical elements of now taking steps in your leadership journey is that you sometimes have to acknowledge what you don't know. Recognizing blind spots is a crucial part of the leadership journey. To navigate transitions successfully, you need people in your life who can help you see the things you might otherwise miss. These people—mentors, coaches, trusted advisors—serve as valuable indicators on your path, helping you course-correct when you start to drift off track. My mother's advice to stop blaming my coach and start taking responsibility for my actions was a wake-up call that forced me to confront my blind spots. Her wisdom helped me see that my resistance to change, rejection of feedback, and loss of confidence were not just personal struggles; but they were also barriers to my growth and success. My mom didn't validate my bad attitude. She gave me an ultimatum: Either I needed to take action and figure it out, or I could go home.

She further admonished me with these words, "If the man tells you to do cartwheels, then you better be the best cartwheel turner on that team. But what I will not stand for is you blaming someone else for actions that you clearly have control over."

I had a decision to make: either put up or pack it up and go home. I knew that I didn't want to go back home. That was not an option. Going home basically meant that I couldn't cut it, that I didn't have what it took to make it.

QUALIFYING YOUR ADVISORS

It's not enough to just have someone point out your blind spots. You also need to be willing to listen and take action. This is where the Faith element of the Blind Exchange Framework comes into play again. Faith requires you to trust the people who are guiding you, to believe that they have your best interests at heart, and to follow their advice, even when it's uncomfortable. Strategies for recognizing and addressing blind spots include actively seeking feedback, being open to criticism, and regularly reflecting on your behavior and decisions. It's also important to qualify your advisors carefully, ensuring they have the relevant leadership experience, a diverse perspective, and a genuine investment in your success. These qualities make them well-equipped to help you see what you might otherwise miss.

RELEVANCE OF THEIR EXPERIENCE

The relevance of an advisor's experience is paramount when it comes to guiding you through transitions and helping you see your blind spots. An advisor with relevant experience has likely faced similar challenges and can offer insights that are directly applicable to your situation. For instance, my mother's experience as an educator and leader meant that she understood the dynamics of change, resistance, and the importance of accountability. She had navigated her own transitions and knew the pitfalls to avoid. Her advice was not theoretical; it was grounded in real-world experience that had been tested over time. When selecting an advisor, consider whether their background aligns with the challenges you are currently facing. Do they have experience in the areas where you need guidance? Can they provide practical strategies that have worked for them or others in similar situations? An advisor with relevant experience can offer more than just encouragement—they can provide actionable advice that is tailored to your specific needs.

LENGTH OF TIME IN THE ROLE

The length of time an advisor has spent in their role or field is another critical factor to consider. Experience is not just about having been through something once; it's about having navigated similar situations repeatedly over time. Advisors with many years in their role have likely seen a wide range of scenarios and have developed a deep understanding of the nuances involved in different situations. They have had the opportunity to refine their approach, learn from their mistakes, and hone their instincts.

This depth of experience allows them to provide more nuanced and insightful advice. For example, an advisor who has spent decades leading teams can offer a level of wisdom that someone newer to the field might not yet possess. They can help you anticipate challenges before they arise and guide you in making decisions that take into account both immediate concerns and long-term implications. The longer an advisor has been in their role, the more likely they are to have a wealth of knowledge and experience that can be invaluable as you navigate your own transitions.

DIVERSITY OF EXPERIENCES

Finally, the diversity of an advisor's experiences plays a crucial role in their ability to offer well-rounded and innovative guidance. Advisors who have worked in various roles, industries, or cultural contexts bring a broader perspective to the table. They are likely to have encountered a wide range of challenges and have developed a more flexible and creative approach to problem-solving. This diversity of experience can be particularly valuable when you are facing complex or unprecedented transitions. For instance, an advisor who has worked in both corporate and nonprofit sectors might offer insights into leadership that are applicable across different environments.

My advisor said what needed to be said to get me back on the right path. After that game and my parents left, I showed up to practice the rest of that year, and I did what I needed to do. I listened to my coach. I embraced the drills, they enhanced my ball-handling skills, and I got better.

I worked harder. I changed my attitude. I embraced change and was more receptive to what my coach had to share. Now, because I had such a bad attitude early on, my coach acquiesced to letting me play in the position where I was more comfortable, the shooting guard position. I was really grateful to him for that. But the perspective my mom helped me to see is what helped me to become better and have more success. As I'll continue to share, it's a critical piece of being a trailblazer. You can't go around pointing the finger at the coach or someone else. You have the power, and your actions determine your success.

Your actions are then determined by your attitude. My change in attitude and change in actions helped me move closer to being the best version of myself. It helped me to get out of my comfort zone.

THE COMFORT ZONE

Remaining in the comfort zone might feel safe, but it comes with significant risks that can hinder personal and professional growth. One of the most insidious dangers of staying in your comfort zone is the stagnation of your skills and abilities. When you consistently operate within a familiar environment, you are less likely to challenge yourself or develop new competencies. This complacency can lead to a gradual erosion of your potential. Over time, you may find that the world around you is changing while you remain stuck in the same place, unprepared for new challenges or opportunities.

In my own experience, staying in my comfort zone meant resisting the transition to a new position on the basketball court. I was comfortable as a shooting guard, where I had experienced success and recognition. The idea of becoming a point guard—an unfamiliar and more demanding role—was intimidating. I feared that I might not excel in this new position, and this fear kept me anchored in my comfort zone. However, by refusing to step out of this familiar role, I was also refusing to expand my skill set and become a more versatile player.

The comfort zone, in this case, became a barrier to my growth, limiting my ability to adapt and succeed in the new environment of college athletics.

Another danger of remaining in the comfort zone is the missed opportunities for personal development and leadership. The comfort zone is often characterized by a lack of challenges, which means there are fewer opportunities to develop resilience, problem-solving skills, and adaptability—qualities that are essential for leadership. When you avoid stepping out of your comfort zone, you miss out on experiences that could help you build these critical skills. For example, had I embraced the challenge of transitioning to a point guard, I might have developed stronger leadership abilities on the court, learning to orchestrate plays and set my teammates up for success. Instead, by clinging to my comfort zone, I missed an opportunity to grow as both a player and a leader.

Finally, staying in your comfort zone can lead to a diminished sense of self-confidence. While it might seem counterintuitive, avoiding challenges and sticking to what is safe can actually weaken your confidence over time. Confidence is built through overcoming obstacles and proving to yourself that you are capable of handling difficult situations. When you stay in your comfort zone, you deprive yourself of these confidence-building experiences. In my case, resisting the transition to point guard eventually led to a loss of confidence in my abilities as a player. I began to doubt myself, not because I had tried and failed but because I had refused to try at all. Instead of being a place of security, the comfort zone became a place where my confidence eroded.

These emotional responses—wanting to stay in my comfort zone, playing the blame game, rejecting feedback, and losing confidence—were closely tied to the elements of Faith in the Blind Exchange Framework. Faith, in this context, is about believing in the process, even when the outcome is uncertain. It's about trusting that the challenges and changes we face are part of a larger plan for our growth and success. However, I struggled with this faith during my transition to college. I wasn't listening to the guidance of my coaches or trusting in their vision for my development. Instead, I was clinging to what I knew, fearful of stepping into the unknown. This resistance to change, lack of faith in the process, and dwindling confidence were obstacles that I had to overcome if I was going to succeed in this new chapter of my life.

A part of my rejection was wanting to stay in my comfort zone. I wanted to just do what I knew I could do, and I didn't want to expand my skill set.

Becoming a better ball handler helped me be a better scorer and a better decision-maker. I was so focused on scoring that sometimes, I would force shots that were not there. There were some scenarios where I needed to make an extra pass to a teammate who was better suited and positioned to score. So, even though I did not make the full transition to being a point guard, I did become a better scorer and a better decision-maker. Opening myself to being out of my comfort zone helped to level up my skill set. I am so glad that I had someone in my life to help me see my blind spots early. If my mom had coddled me and vilified my coach, I would not have achieved the success that I have. As you continue to start thinking about your own journey and your comfort zone, reflect on who's in your life who is trying to help provide you with the perspective you need to level up. Who's in your life trying to help provide you with the perspective to help you take action that will lead toward your success?

Toward the middle of freshman year, I eventually got to the seventh player coming off the bench, and while I did not start, at least I was now getting playing time and doing a little bit better. I had found a way to contribute to my team. In my post-season meeting with my coach, he gave me a fair critique. He was disappointed that I was not more open to the point guard position, but he did see that I had improved as a shooting guard and was okay with me staying in my comfort zone, being a good teammate, and contributing to the team as a shooting guard. He acknowledged that I had made progress and invited me to return for my sophomore year.

But there were a couple of things he asked of me. First, he wanted me to attend summer school because he felt like that would help me stay on track to graduate on time. Second, it was an opportunity for me to continue to develop my skills and work on my game. It was a great chance. Because my attitude changed, my coach's attitude had changed toward me as well. I felt like we were developing a more positive relationship that would be better suited and beneficial for me moving forward to SUCCESS! I was able to keep my scholarship and return for my sophomore year.

Sophomore season was *lit*. We finished as one of the top three teams that year. I was selected to be a captain of the team. I made the Western Junior College Athletic Conference (WJCAC) All-Star team. I led the team in steals and was named the most valuable defensive player at our team awards banquet. It was really a culmination of all the hard work I had put in once I adjusted my attitude and became more open to the possibilities and opportunities for me to expand my game. Even at my graduation, I received the Vera Sue Spencer Award, an award given to someone who has excelled in representing the university overall (academically, athletically, and civically). It was awarded to one student out of the entire graduating class. I felt like it was the reward for making those adjustments and becoming the best version of myself. Within those two years, my ball-handling skills were better. I was a little bit stronger now that I had participated in a full strength and conditioning program. I felt like I was fully prepared with the tools to transition into my final two years as a college student-athlete.

FORESHADOWING

But something was still missing. I was the state triple jump champion, and I still had a desire to participate in track.

One day during the spring of my sophomore year, my roommate and I decided to go out to the track to see if we still had it. She told me that she was a hurdler, and I told her I was a state triple jump champion. I was convinced that the rigorous strength and conditioning program we had been participating in had surely given me what I needed to jump 40 feet. I remembered my steps and took a chance to see how far I could jump. I quickly got out of the pit, looked intently at the distance I had jumped, and declared that I had jumped 40 feet. I was sure of it. The only problem was we didn't have a tape measure to verify the distance. It didn't matter though. As far as I was concerned, I had jumped 40 feet, and no one could tell me different.

CONCLUSION

Transitioning from high school to college was not just about moving to a new environment; it was a crucial step in blazing my own trail. This chapter has delved into the intricacies of managing such a pivotal transition, emphasizing how essential it is to step out of the comfort zone, embrace feedback, and maintain confidence—even when the path ahead is uncertain. The shift from the familiar grounds of high school athletics to the more competitive and demanding world of college sports required me to re-examine who I was as an athlete, a student, and an individual. The challenges of resisting change, rejecting feedback, and losing confidence were not just obstacles—they were tests of my ability to forge my own path.

One of the core lessons from this chapter is the inherent danger of staying within the confines of the comfort zone. While it might seem like a safe haven, remaining too long in what is familiar can lead to stagnation and prevent us from realizing our true potential. For those who aspire to blaze their own trail, the comfort zone is not a place of growth but a barrier that must be overcome. Additionally, this chapter highlighted the indispensable role of trusted advisors in navigating these transitions. By choosing advisors with relevant experience, significant time in their roles, and a diverse range of experiences, you can gain the insight needed to identify and address your blind spots, helping you to stay on course as you chart your unique path.

As I navigated the transition from being a high school standout to a college freshman, I discovered that true trailblazing requires a willingness to embrace the unfamiliar, to be open to constructive criticism, and to trust the process, even when the outcome is uncertain. These lessons were vital in helping me adjust my mindset and approach, ultimately enabling me to succeed both on and off the court.

In Chapter 5, we will continue the journey of blazing your own trail by exploring the strategies and mindsets necessary to navigate transitions effectively. We will delve deeper into how adaptability and resilience are crucial for overcoming setbacks and staying on course. Blazing your own trail is not a one-time event but an ongoing process of realignment and recalibration. As we move forward, we will examine how the lessons learned from past transitions can be leveraged to navigate future challenges, ensuring that each step you take strengthens your path toward your ultimate goals. The journey of a trailblazer is filled with uncertainties, but with the right tools and mindset, you can turn every challenge into an opportunity to forge ahead with confidence and purpose.

5
EMBRACING COMPETITION AND PREPARATION

THE DREAM OF DIVISION I BASKETBALL

From the moment I first picked up a basketball, I dreamed of playing at the NCAA Division I level. To me, playing Division I basketball represented the pinnacle of achievement in the sport, especially at a time when there were no professional women's basketball leagues in the United States. The thought of being recognized as one of the top players in the country fueled my desire to reach this level, and I was determined to make it happen. I had several opportunities to attend smaller schools, but they didn't align with my vision. I needed to test myself against the best, and eventually, that led me to the University of New Orleans (UNO).

One of the reasons I chose UNO was because Louisiana Tech University (LaTech) and UNO were members of the Sun Belt Conference, an NCAA Division I mid-major conference. But LaTech would have been considered almost a professional team. They were one of the top four teams every year. The Lady Techsters, coached by the legendary Leon Barmore, and the Lady Vols of the University of Tennessee, coached by Pat Summitt, were the torchbearers, the trailblazers for college women's basketball programs. If you wanted to say you were a top player, you wanted to go to LaTech or Tennessee. I wanted the opportunity to compete against the best.

I had a personal vendetta against LaTech because my hometown, Minden, Louisiana, was about 30 miles east on I-20 towards Ruston, Louisiana. When I graduated from high school, I didn't even get a recruitment letter from them. It's almost as if all of the hard work, making it to the semifinals of the Louisiana High School State Association (LHSAA) Sweet 16 Tournament two years in a row, and being the leading scorer on the team meant nothing.

In addition, I was also an All-State First Team player two years in a row—an All-Star team selection—and I didn't even receive a letter saying, "Hey, we might be interested in you becoming a Lady Techster." I felt disrespected. Part of my choosing UNO was also the opportunity to go up against one of the top programs in the country and really see if I had what it took to be considered a top player in the conference. I thought, We are going to get a chance to play them twice a year, and this is going to be my opportunity to see if I measure up. It was great! It was probably one of the best decisions I have ever made.

TRAILBLAZERS AREN'T AFRAID OF COMPETITION

Blazing your own trail often means confronting the competition head-on rather than shying away from it. I was still playing shooting guard, as I shared in Chapter 4, even though my previous coach thought that point guard would be a better fit for me at an NCAA Division I school. As you know, I settled on being a shooting guard. By this point, I had improved my ball-handling skills, and now it was time to put up or shut up.

I'll never forget finally squaring up against LaTech in my junior year. It was such an amazing game. For me, facing LaTech represented the ultimate challenge. I wasn't content with just playing the game; I wanted to test my skills against the best and see if I truly had what it took. We did not beat them in my junior year, but the experience was invaluable. It set the stage for what would come in my senior year when we finally defeated them in one of the most memorable games of my college career.

We beat LaTech on January 11, 1997. I scored 11 points in that game. In fact, I scored the final points that secured our victory 66 to 63. It was not just a personal triumph but a validation of all the hard work, preparation, and belief that had brought me to that moment. To this day, it's one of the most significant wins over a highly-ranked opponent for the UNO Lady Privateer Women's Basketball Program.

Beating LaTech was a defining moment in my journey. It proved to me that I was capable of achieving my goals, even when the odds were stacked against me. It also reinforced the idea that to blaze your own trail, you must be willing to step into the arena, face your fears, and compete with everything you have. This mentality is what sets trailblazers apart—they are not afraid of competition; they seek it out, knowing that it will bring out the best in them.

RETURN TO TRACK AND FIELD

One of the unique aspects of my college experience was the opportunity to pursue both of my athletic passions—basketball and track and field. After two years of focusing on basketball, I was eager to return to track and field, where I had once been a state champion in the triple jump. The idea of balancing both sports was daunting, but it was also incredibly exciting. I approached my basketball coach with the idea, and to my delight, he was supportive. He saw the potential for track and field to enhance my basketball performance, and I saw it as a chance to reconnect with a sport that had brought me so much joy and success in the past.

Returning to track and field was not without its challenges. I had not competed in the sport for two years, and I knew that I would need to work hard to regain my form. When I first approached the track coach, I could sense his skepticism. He questioned whether I could achieve the ambitious goal I had set for myself—jumping 40 feet in the triple jump. But I was determined to prove him wrong. I knew that the strength and conditioning work I had done for basketball would serve me well, and I was confident that with hard work and perseverance, I could reach my goal.

Basketball season was over, and I was excited to see the track coach.

I had gotten approval from my basketball coach. I said to him, "Hey coach, I can jump 40 feet."

He looked at me and asked, "Well, what is your personal record, your PR? What is the furthest you've jumped?"

I said, "In high school, I won the state triple jump, and I jumped 36 feet, four inches."

He looked at me, and it was almost as if he was thinking, Huh? She's just talking. I could tell he was doubting my ability to jump 40 feet. Add to that I hadn't competed in track and field for two years, and he wasn't convinced.

I remember thinking, Why doesn't he believe me? I know I can jump 40 feet. I jumped 36 feet, 4 inches, without a strength and conditioning program. Now, I had been in a strength and conditioning program for three years. In my mind, the logic made perfect sense. If I could do 36'–4" without strength and conditioning, then adding three years of strength and conditioning should equal jumping 40 feet. At least, that's how I saw it.

I remember going out to my first week of practice, and I remember not getting much attention from the coach. I showed up, and I said, "Hey, coach, I'm here. I'm excited to participate this year." He had given me some workouts, and he put me on a relay team.

I was excited to join the 4x400m relay team. I ran the open 200m run, and I also did the triple jump. But I was a little frustrated because I felt the coach didn't believe in my abilities.

"WALK IT LIKE YOU TALK IT"—MIGOS

One of the most important lessons I learned during this time was the value of backing up your words with action. It's one thing to tell people what you're capable of, but it's another thing entirely to show them. I had set the goal of jumping 40 feet, and I knew that I needed to put in the work to make it happen. Week after week, I trained hard, pushing myself to improve. After just four meets, I achieved my goal, breaking the school record with a jump of 40 feet—a record that still stands to this day.

This experience reinforced the idea that trailblazers must not only have confidence and faith in themselves but also the discipline and determination to follow through on their goals. It's not enough to talk about what you want to achieve; you have to be willing to do the work necessary to make it a reality. By setting ambitious goals and relentlessly pursuing them, you can break through barriers and reach new heights. I also understood the importance of actually backing that up at some point. And sometimes, you have to pop out and show'em - like Kendrick Lamar said.

I will never forget Coach's response. It was like a Chariots of Fire moment, as if in slow motion with the music in the background. He raised his hands up, kind of in a victory formation, and started running towards me. He got to me, picked me up, spun me around, and all of a sudden, I became like the superstar. He assigned a coach to me from that point to start working with me, because if I could continue to get better with my technique, there was a potential that I could qualify for the Olympic trials within the next few years. I thought it was one thing when you shared with someone what you could do, but it's another thing to actually get it done. The first cornerstone of being able to show people what you're capable of is having confidence and faith/belief in yourself. We discussed in Chapter 1 how that is a foundational principle for leadership. Belief, confidence, and faith are first. You have to believe that it actually can happen. The second foundational principle we talked about is preparation: You have to do the work. Even though I hadn't been on a track for two years, I had been working to develop and strengthen my muscles thanks to the strength and conditioning program. For two years, I had been strengthening my body. I was stronger and faster. I was certainly prepared for this moment.

So, I believed in myself, and I knew I was prepared in terms of strength and conditioning to actually achieve that success.

Another goal had been met. I was checking them off one by one.

- Beat LaTech: ☑
- Jump 40 feet and set the school record: ☑

Fast forward to my final year of graduation. The final thing that I wanted to do was graduate within four years. At that time, there was conversation about student-athletes not being able to complete their academic obligations within four years. There were even conversations around some students just going to college to play sports and not even finishing their college degree. Well, I was very intent on not being a statistic.

THE WNBA TRYOUT

For me, basketball was a means to an end. As I said in the previous chapter, there was no professional women's basketball league in the United States. As far as I was concerned, there was no reason for me to aim to play professional basketball when it didn't exist in the U.S. So, I needed to focus on finishing my degree, preparing to get a job, and starting my career. As my senior year was coming to an end, everything was in alignment. I had passed nine hours during summer school, and I was ready to walk, completing my final year and graduating within four years, which would be my final accomplishment.

As I was approaching graduation and contemplating what was next for me, I received a call from my coach. I was somewhat uneasy by the end of my senior year. I hadn't had the opportunity to do many internships in my career of interest, which was Communications. Internships are the equivalent of practice; they're how you learn and develop your skill set. I always wanted to do TV, like Oprah. I wanted to have a show through which I could make a positive impact on the world. Even though I had the book knowledge and I passed my communication courses, I didn't feel prepared to walk into a TV studio and begin a career in TV. I began to have some apprehension about what was next, what I was going to do, and if I was really ready. Was I prepared to go into a TV studio or a newsroom and begin to do that work?

But something interesting happened that year. Rumors were circulating about the formation of a women's professional basketball league in the U.S., the WNBA, the Women's National Basketball Association. This was a dream I hadn't even allowed myself to consider because it simply didn't exist when I started my college career. But now, as I was preparing to graduate, the possibility of playing professional basketball in my own country was suddenly within reach.

At the end of the semester, as I was preparing for graduation, Coach called me into his office and told me that two teams were interested in having me try out: the Houston Comets and the Charlotte Sting. I was thrilled. The chance to play in the WNBA was something I never expected, and I was eager to seize the opportunity. I chose to try out for the Houston Comets, not only because they were closer to home, but also because I wanted my family to be able to see me play. Driving to Houston was no different than driving to New Orleans, except they were going southwest instead of going southeast. It made perfect sense that I would go to Houston and try out for a women's professional basketball league that was going to be happening right here in the United States.

The tryouts were amazing. I was so excited.

I was stronger. I was faster. I was a better ball handler. I could score the ball. Even though I was still considered somewhat undersized for my position as a shooting guard, I knew I was playing some of the best basketball I had ever played. I remember being so grateful for all of the additional support, coaching, and skill development that I had received from all of my coaches.

Tryouts started off with about 50 to 75 people. In the first round of cuts, they cut half the people, leaving about 25 to 40 of us.

I remember thinking, Okay, I made it through round one. Now it's time to turn it up a notch in the second round. I was playing some of the best basketball I'd ever played. I was making good decisions with the basketball. I was scoring when I was supposed to score. I was not turning the ball over. Unfortunately, I didn't make it past the second round. I got cut.

I was devastated.

I just couldn't understand how I could play so well and not make it on to that next round. I finally got back and reflected on how cool it was to know that I had the opportunity to try out for the inaugural season of the WNBA, even though that was never my goal. I still thought it was really cool that I had a couple of scouts look at my film, say that they thought I could play professional basketball, and invite me to come and try out. A week or so after the tryout, I went to visit Coach and said, "Hey Coach, I wanted to know if you received any feedback from the scouts? I'd like to know why I got cut." As he sat there and proceeded to provide me with feedback, he said the scouts were really impressed with my scoring ability. They thought that I defended really well.

I was really quick. I was athletic. He said, "Unfortunately, they were looking for a point guard!" The disappointment was crushing, but it also led to a critical reflection on my journey.

THE IMPORTANCE OF PREPARATION

When he said that they were looking for a point guard, my heart just dropped. It took me back to my freshman year when my coach said to me, "I really think your skills would be better suited for this position." All I kept saying was, "I don't even know why he's making me do this. It's not like there's a women's professional basketball league anyway." The lesson that I learned was that I was not prepared for the next-level position, like the point guard level, because I had rejected every opportunity to embrace that new role. Every time my coach put me in that position, I basically said, "No, I don't want to do it, nor any of the work to be prepared to succeed in that position." I did very well as a shooting guard, but when the opportunity was available, they weren't looking for a shooting guard. They were looking for a point guard.

Sometimes, those advisors that you have in your life have foresight that can help position you for your next level. That's why it's critical that you be open to other possibilities. Your willingness to buy into those processes is what makes those possibilities now an opportunity and a reality for you. I was not prepared when the opportunity presented itself.

Because I was not prepared, I did not reap the benefits. As I noted earlier, you can't know everything. It is a fundamental truth that you must accept if you want to blaze your own trail. But guess what? Here's the good news. You don't have to know everything. You have to be open to the processes and the possibilities that you could be more, that you could transition and do something on another level if you're willing to do the work and prepare. As I shared, even though I had become more skilled at the position I played, the position of shooting guard, the position where I was comfortable, I could not advance in the basketball world. And what we don't want to be is in a place where we get stuck, and we're not able to level up.

To blaze your own trail, you have to be willing to do something outside of your comfort zone. While we cannot predict the future, we can most certainly be prepared. We have to do everything we can to ensure our best success moving forward by being prepared for those opportunities.

Preparation is the thing that levels you up. When you can't know, and you can't predict what is next, preparation is the key. What I've learned as I've walked through my particular path is that trailblazers don't know, but they have faith/confidence in themselves, and they aren't afraid to listen, trust, and prepare. When they lose focus, they activate the Triple-A Method and act swiftly, taking the steps that will allow them to be prepared and open to other possibilities. This story was the final step in my understanding and the last lesson I needed before launching out on my own to pursue a career.

Learning, after the tryouts, that the team was looking for a point guard was a tough pill to swallow. I realized that my refusal to embrace the point guard role had cost me a once-in-a-lifetime opportunity. This experience underscored the importance of being open to change, adapting to new roles, and always being prepared for the unexpected.

Blazing your own trail requires not only setting ambitious goals but also being adaptable and prepared to seize opportunities when they arise. You may not always know what the future holds, but by being open to new possibilities and willing to put in the work to prepare for them, you can position yourself for success. This experience taught me that preparation is key and that being open to new roles and challenges can open doors you never knew existed.

CONCLUSION

The journey from my freshman to senior year in college was filled with transitions, challenges, and triumphs. Each step along the way taught me valuable lessons about what it means to blaze your own trail. I learned that to be a trailblazer, you must have confidence in yourself, be willing to face competition, pursue multiple passions, and, most importantly, be adaptable and prepared for whatever opportunities come your way. The experiences I had during these years were not just about playing sports; they were about preparing for life and leadership.

As I graduated from college and prepared to step into uncharted territory, I carried with me the lessons I had learned on the court and the track. These lessons would guide me as I moved forward into my career, helping me to continue blazing my own trail in whatever path I chose to pursue. In the next chapter, we will explore how these lessons continued to shape my journey as I transitioned from college to the professional world, where the stakes were higher and the challenges even greater.

PART 3

CATALYST TO BLAZING YOUR OWN TRAIL

6

FORESIGHT AND FAILURE

*"I once was lost, but now I'm found.
Was blind, but now I see."*
– Amazing Grace

As I look back on the years from age 10 to 22, I see a path marked by pivotal moments, significant challenges, and triumphs that have shaped who I am today. From the early days of idolizing Flo-Jo and striving to win my first race to the high school years where I juggled basketball, track, and cheerleading, and then on to the intense and competitive environment of college athletics —each experience was a stepping stone that prepared me for what lay ahead. These years were more than just a series of events; they were a training ground where I learned to develop foresight and discover my purpose.

The process of reflection is critical because it allows us to connect the dots between past experiences and future aspirations. By examining the challenges I faced and the triumphs I achieved, I can see how each moment was a piece of a larger puzzle—one that I am still piecing together today. This chapter will explore the lessons learned during these formative years, focusing on how they have informed my approach to leadership, decision-making, and personal growth. These lessons are not just memories of past achievements and setbacks—they are the anchors that have allowed me to develop the foresight needed to navigate my career.

FORESIGHT AND THE BLIND EXCHANGE FRAMEWORK

Foresight is the ability to predict what will happen or be needed in the future. Foresight is a powerful tool that allows you to anticipate challenges, plan strategically, and navigate your path with purpose. To truly blaze your own trail, you must develop the ability to see beyond the immediate and envision the bigger picture. Foresight is guided by the key principles of the Blind Exchange Framework: *faith, focus,* and *forward momentum* to navigate transitions and overcome failure.

FORESIGHT AND FAITH

Faith is the foundation that enables you to move forward with confidence, even when the path ahead is unclear. It provides clarity of vision, allowing you to trust in your ability to navigate the unknown. In the Blind Exchange Framework, faith is about trusting the process and relying on your instincts, even when you can't see the entire path. It's about listening to that inner voice and having the courage to act on it, knowing that your preparation and intuition will guide you to success.

When I dropped the baton during that critical race, it was a moment of failure that shook my confidence. I had lost faith in the process we had practiced and doubted my own instincts. This lapse in faith led to a moment of hesitation, causing me to look back and lose focus. The lesson here is profound: without faith, your vision becomes clouded, and you are more likely to falter. Faith clears the fog of doubt and hesitation, enabling you to see your path more clearly. It empowers you to act decisively, trusting that your preparation and intuition will guide you to success.

In the context of the Blind Exchange Framework, faith is essential because it anchors you in the present while allowing you to project into the future. It gives you the confidence to make bold decisions, knowing that even if you can't see the entire path, each step forward will reveal the next. This clarity of vision is crucial when navigating transitions and overcoming obstacles. When you have faith, you are more likely to stay focused on your long-term goals, even when faced with setbacks.

FORESIGHT, FOCUS, AND FORWARD MOMENTUM

In the pursuit of success, it's easy to get caught up in the minutiae and lose sight of the big picture. However, maintaining a focus on your overarching goals is essential for long-term success. Foresight is about seeing beyond the immediate challenges and keeping your eyes on the prize. Within the Blind Exchange Framework, focus represents the discipline to stay committed to your path, despite distractions and setbacks.

During that fateful race, my focus shifted from the big picture goal —winning the state championship—to the immediate concern of how others were performing. I allowed myself to be distracted by my competitors, which led to a critical mistake. This experience taught me the importance of staying true to your own journey and not being swayed by external factors. Success comes from staying focused on your goals and trusting in the process that got you there.

Focusing on the big picture doesn't mean ignoring the details; rather, it means keeping those details in context. It's about understanding that every step you take, every action you make, is part of a larger plan. When you focus on the big picture, you're better able to navigate setbacks because you see them as temporary obstacles rather than insurmountable barriers. This mindset allows you to stay motivated and continue pushing forward with momentum, even when things don't go as planned.

KEY LESSONS IN FORESIGHT Lessons in Foresight

- **Listening and Trusting Advisors**

One of the most powerful lessons in foresight came from learning to listen to those who had my best interests at heart. My mother, in particular, played a pivotal role in helping me see what I could not. When I blamed my coach for my lack of playing time, it was my mother who made me realize that the real issue was within me. By listening to her and accepting her guidance, I was able to identify my blind spots and make the necessary adjustments. This experience taught me that true foresight often comes from trusting the wisdom of those who can see what we cannot.

- **Adapting to Change**

Foresight also involves the ability to adapt to change. During my freshman year in college, I resisted the idea of transitioning to a point guard position. I was comfortable as a shooting guard, and the thought of changing roles felt daunting. But as I look back, I realize that this resistance was a short-sighted response to a challenge that could have prepared me for even greater opportunities—like the WNBA tryouts, where a point guard position was exactly what was needed. Adapting to change is not just about accepting new roles; it's about seeing the long-term benefits of stepping out of your comfort zone.

- **Maintaining Focus Amidst Distractions**

The importance of focus is another critical lesson in foresight. In leadership, as in life, distractions are inevitable. The key is to maintain focus on your goals, even when external factors threaten to derail you. During the state championship relay, my decision to look back instead of focusing on the finish line caused us to lose the race. This mistake underscored the need to keep my eyes on the ultimate goal, no matter what distractions arose. Maintaining focus ensures that you stay on course, enabling you to foresee potential challenges and navigate them effectively.

UNDERSTANDING FORESIGHT THROUGH FAILURE

Foresight is often born out of failure. Failure is an inevitable part of any journey, but how you respond to it determines your ultimate success. When things don't go as planned, we are forced to reassess our circumstances, reflect on our decisions, and recalibrate our path forward. One of the first lessons I learned in developing foresight was that failure makes you reassess your circumstances. After I dropped the baton during a crucial relay race, I replayed the exchange over and over in my mind. Why did I look back instead of trusting the process we had practiced? This moment of failure was not just a mistake; it was a revelation. It revealed to me that I lacked faith in the process and, more importantly, in myself.

The Blind Exchange Framework teaches us that in moments of critical decision-making, we must listen and act with confidence, not rely only on what we see. My decision to look back was a physical manifestation of a deeper issue—a lack of faith. I learned that in many situations, you won't have the luxury of looking back; you will need to trust that what you're hearing, your instincts, and your preparation are enough to guide you forward. This kind of trust is foundational to developing foresight because it enables you to move with conviction, even when the path ahead is unclear.

FAILURE PREPARES YOU FOR YOUR NEXT LEVEL

Another lesson I learned is that failure prepares you for *your* next level. While I had dropped the baton due to a lack of faith and focus, the race was not over. I had two choices: either leave the baton on the ground and wallow in my failure, or pick up the baton, move forward, and finish the race. I chose to move forward. This is probably the most critical lesson that I learned, and I consider it the foundation for anyone who has had success. You must muster enough strength to pick yourself up and continue to move forward. It would have been easy for me to give up, but here's the reality: I still had three more events to compete in that day. Moving forward signaled my acknowledgment of my failure but also my determination to move forward mentally if I was going to reach the next level. The next level that day was to do my absolute best in the three remaining events in hopes of becoming a state champion in at least one event.

In my reassessment, I activated my faith, refocused on the processes that had brought me to the state championship meet, and moved forward with a renewed commitment to do my very best. As a result, I achieved my goal of becoming a state champion. I won the triple jump competition and finished third in the high jump that day. My ability to learn these critical lessons from failure set the foundation that has helped me to have consistent success throughout my career.

This experience taught me that failure is not the end, but rather a stepping stone to the next level of growth and achievement. When you experience failure, it is important to reassess your circumstances, understand that you are not perfect and that faith is a requirement, focus on perfecting your processes rather than just the end goal, and you will be ready to move forward to your next level. Armed with these lessons, I headed off to college to begin my journey into independence.

FAILURE GIVES YOU PERSPECTIVE

Failure has a unique way of offering perspective, and this was a lesson I learned early on. Perspective often refers to how you see something or your point of view on a situation or topic. Failure in this situation forced me to examine the attitudes and actions that had taken place during my four years as a college athlete, which led me to this point. When I arrived at South Plains College (SPC), my coach saw that I had great potential and that, with some work, I could transition to the point guard position. Unfortunately, I did not have the proper attitude. My perspective at that time was that since there was no professional women's league in the United States, it would be a waste of my time to invest any additional energy to advance my skill set. My talent at the shooting guard position was good enough to play at the college level.

My goal was to complete my college career with no debt, and that was good enough for me. What a limited perspective! My perspective on this situation is what set up this whole failure. Because I didn't commit to advancing my skill set, I was not ready when the opportunity presented itself.

You've heard the old cliché that luck is when "preparation meets opportunity." Well, I certainly was not prepared, and it was all my fault. When I dug a little deeper into what I was going through as a college freshman, I realized that not only did I have a limited perspective, but I was also intimidated by the challenge. I was scared that I would fail and lose my scholarship. When we do not have strategies for how to deal with our fears, it can derail us. I remember calling home and blaming my coaches when things were not going well for me. It was easy to put the blame on my coach because I did not have to look in the mirror and be accountable.

Geesh! I was so mad at Mom that night. I felt like she had turned her back on me and that she did not really care about me. However, that was far from the truth. She had given me one of the most important lessons of my life: that with a change in perspective, I had the POWER to change my circumstances. I eventually figured it out (lol) and became a better player and teammate. What changed, you ask? MY PERSPECTIVE.

In becoming a better player and teammate, I began to establish stronger relationships with not only my teammates but also my coaches. They learned to trust me in the role that I accepted, and I was able to deliver consistently in practice and on the court. The change in MY PERSPECTIVE equaled a change in my BEHAVIOR. The change in my BEHAVIOR shaped the perceptions of my coaches and teammates, who depended on me to do my part to ensure our team would have success. Because YOUR BEHAVIOR is your BRAND, it further speaks to the importance of using failure to shape your perspective. At the end of the day, the only person/thing you have control over is your PERSPECTIVE and your BEHAVIOR.

How you process and make meaning of difficulties, obstacles, and challenges influences your perspective. Challenges and obstacles are integral to growth. They may bring on elements of fear, but they are necessary, and the better you understand this concept, the better chance you will have at overcoming your fears. Because of the fear of failure, I had an extremely limited perspective, lost an opportunity to grow and expand my skill set, and when the opportunity of a lifetime presented itself, I was not ready. However, I had taken steps to become an asset to my team in the role that I accepted, and little did I know that those changes to my behavior would create alternate possibilities after losing out on the WNBA opportunity.

FAILURE MAKES YOU AWARE OF ALTERNATE POSSIBILITIES

After missing out on the opportunity of a lifetime, I was pretty bummed. It was common for me to enter into a post-season depression after my sports seasons would end. Now that this opportunity was no longer available, I began looking for other possibilities. I had a year of track eligibility remaining, so there was an opportunity to return to UNO and begin working on a master's degree. After all, I was not ready to go into the real world. Internship opportunities were tough to commit to due to our basketball schedule. I was ready to graduate but did not have experience. I knew this would make it hard for me to get a job. Have you ever been there? Felt lost? Didn't know what direction to take? I used to dream of participating in the Olympics. Maybe returning to run track would be a great idea.

I had developed a good relationship with my urban studies professor, and he thought I would be a good candidate for the dual Masters of Public Administration/Juris Doctorate program that was a collaboration between the University of New Orleans and Loyola/Tulane. My coach had visited with me regarding a graduate assistantship with the basketball team if I was interested. It looked like there would still be alternate possibilities for me.

Here is the twist: Although I had not been willing to expand my basketball skill set, I had developed strong relationships with both my coaches and professors. What I did not realize at that time was my BEHAVIORS were being evaluated by every action I took. Whether I showed up on time for practice, what kind of mentality/attitude I brought to practice, or how I carried myself around campus when my coaches were not around—all of these behaviors were being watched. I had gained the trust of my coaches, and as a result, not only did I earn a starting position, but I also earned a role as captain of the team. When the WNBA opportunity did not work out for me, my head coach was led to extend an opportunity for me to work with him as a graduate assistant. Unfortunately, I needed a break from basketball, so I declined the opportunity. I graduated from the University of New Orleans with my Bachelor of General Studies degree and headed back home to spend some time with my family and gain some clarity on my next steps.

This is a key step in how failure fuels success. Sometimes, you need to take a step back after gaining a better perspective and then examine your alternate possibilities so that you can chart your next move. It was around mid-June, and I was beginning to feel anxious about my next steps. It is quite common to feel anxious or nervous once you receive that diploma. Doubt runs through your mind. You wonder whether you have what it takes. Are you really prepared to begin a professional career? I knew I was not ready to begin a professional career, but graduate school was my desire, and if all else failed, I said my prayers and kept looking for alternate possibilities.

That's when I received a phone call from my recruiting coach. She had left a year ago to take a head coaching position at the University of Louisiana at Lafayette (ULL). She was looking for a graduate assistant to complete her staff. She thought I would be a great fit because she remembered I was a positive person and a hard worker, and she thought I would be a great role model for the kind of young ladies she wanted to build the program. She shared that ULL had a master's degree in Communications. If I accepted the opportunity, they would pay for my degree, and I would serve as a graduate assistant for the women's basketball team. I was thrilled. Not only would I get to stay connected to a sport that I loved, but I would finally have the opportunity to get some experience in TV and maybe eventually have my own show. WRONG. This opportunity set me on a path to fulfillment that would far exceed my dreams or expectations.

What made this opportunity so special was the fact that when the coach spoke to me about the qualities she was looking for, I realized that I was totally prepared. While I had shunned the role of becoming a point guard, I had always accepted the role of being an ambassador and leader. During my four years in college, I served in many similar capacities (Presidential ambassador at South Plains College, team captain, public speaker, etc.). Anytime there was a need for the women's basketball program to be represented, I was always given the assignment. Was I nervous? YES. I was always nervous when I had to speak in front of others or represent our athletics department or school as a whole, but I did it anyway. I had no idea that serving in those capacities was preparing me for the path that God had pre-destined for me.

I was so excited about the opportunity that I did not want to squander it. I took the lessons of failure from the past eight years to help me navigate the new challenge of transitioning from undergraduate to graduate school and from player to coach.

HOW FORESIGHT AND PURPOSE INTERSECT

- **Finding Purpose Through Challenges**

Purpose is not something that is always clear from the outset; it often emerges through the challenges we face and the lessons we learn. For me, each setback and success helped clarify what truly mattered to me in my life and career. Whether it was the disappointment of not making the WNBA or the triumph of beating La Tech, each experience brought me closer to understanding my purpose.

- **Aligning Actions with Purpose**

One of the most significant lessons I learned was the importance of aligning my actions with my purpose. This alignment became a guiding force in every decision I made. For instance, when I chose to pursue basketball over track, it wasn't just about the sport—I was aligning myself with a purpose that involved being part of a team, leading by example, and pushing myself to achieve greatness. This alignment between purpose and action is what fuels persistence and keeps you motivated, even when the path is difficult.

- **Purpose as a Driving Force**

Purpose is not just a guiding principle; it is a driving force that propels you forward, especially in moments of doubt or uncertainty. During the most challenging times—whether it was navigating the transition to college, dealing with the pressure of competition, or facing the disappointment of not making the WNBA—my sense of purpose kept me going. It was the understanding that I was not just playing a game or pursuing a career; I was living out a purpose that was bigger than any single event or outcome. This sense of purpose is what allows you to rise above setbacks and continue pursuing your goals with determination and resilience.

- **Connecting the Dots**

Foresight and purpose are not isolated concepts; they are deeply interconnected. Foresight allows you to anticipate and prepare for future challenges, while purpose gives you the motivation and direction to navigate those challenges. Together, they create a powerful framework for success. By understanding how these elements work together, I was able to make decisions that were not only strategic but also deeply meaningful.

CONCLUSION: SETTING THE STAGE FOR WHAT'S NEXT

As I prepare for the next phase of my journey, I carry with me the lessons of foresight and purpose. These lessons have not only shaped who I am today but will continue to guide me as I navigate the challenges and opportunities that lie ahead. In the chapters to come, I will explore how these principles have been applied in my career and how they have helped me to continue blazing my own trail.

I encourage you to take a moment to reflect on your own journey. What lessons have you learned that have helped you develop foresight? What challenges have clarified your purpose? As you continue on your path, remember that foresight and purpose are powerful tools that can help you navigate even the most uncertain of times. They are the anchors that keep you grounded, the compass that guides you forward, and the fuel that powers your journey.

Blazing your own trail is not just about achieving success; it's about understanding where you are going and why you are going there. It's about seeing beyond the immediate and staying true to what truly matters. As you move forward, let foresight and purpose be your guide, and you will find that the path you create will be one of meaning, impact, and lasting fulfillment.

PART 4

BENEFITS OF BLAZING YOUR OWN TRAIL

7
THE PATH REVEALED

Man, what an amazing journey from fifth grade to college. The lessons I learned were so critical in helping me figure out how to navigate a path that is unknown. I graduated from college, missed an opportunity to be an inaugural player for the Women's National Basketball Association (WNBA), and now I was forced to think about what's next. It was the summer of 1997, and I was contemplating what my next move would be.

We arranged for an official campus visit to ULL, which included meetings with key staff members and an assessment of housing accommodations. During the visit, I met with members of the graduate Communications program, and my meeting with the Dean of the Communications program sealed the deal. After weighing my options and still having a desire to pursue a career in media/TV, I decided that pursuing a master's in Communication was the right choice. This decision meant I would be stepping away from the Olympic track dream, but it seemed like a logical step toward achieving my goal of eventually being on TV. Now that I had assumed the role of graduate assistant basketball coach, I wouldn't have the same level of responsibilities that I had as a student-athlete, and I would finally get the experiences I needed to have a career in television.

At the end of the visit, the coach shared what the benefits would include:

1. They would pay for my tuition.
2. I was going to be given housing.
3. A meal plan and a small stipend of $4,500 per year, paid over a 10-month period ($450 per month).

So, while I wasn't going to make much money, my accommodation was free, and my school tuition was covered. This totally made sense, right? I'd be getting my communications degree, finding some way to get on TV, and they were going to pay for school—perfect!

I was excited about this decision because now I was getting closer to the thing I said I wanted to do. I let my track coach know that I appreciated the opportunity he extended to me for an additional year, but that I was going to go ahead and pursue this Communications master's degree because this was going to put me on the path to finally doing what I really wanted to do—be on TV.

I moved to Lafayette, LA, and got accepted into the master's program. The coach sat with me, gave me my job description, and walked through each bullet point of all the things I would be responsible for. I'd never been a coach, so there was a lot that I had to learn. I remember being super excited, thinking, *Okay, this is going to be great.* I was going to be responsible for player development, operations, recruiting, and summer camp. There were a lot of things in that job description that were pretty cool and really exciting.

School started in August, and our first recruiting class arrived on campus. In our first team meeting, the coach introduced me to those young ladies as "Coach Kiki." At that moment, I realized this was the path for me. The young ladies approached me as if I had all this wisdom. I could see their hope and excitement in learning from me. I had just graduated, yet these young ladies looked to me for direction. I was somewhat flabbergasted, unable to understand how I had gone from being a player just a few months ago to now being called "Coach," with them looking to me for guidance. All I could think was, *This is where I'm supposed to be. This is the path I'm supposed to take.*

Even though when I made my decision to go there, it was about the communications degree and having this opportunity to get some experience to be on TV, at the moment those young ladies were looking for direction from me, I knew this was the path I was supposed to be on. I felt a deep responsibility to walk well in front of them, ensuring I was a good leader and setting a positive example, rather than simply telling them what they needed to do. It was important to me, just as it was when I was a student-athlete. When I was named captain of the team and selected by my peers, they expected me to be someone they could depend on—to do the right thing and be accountable for the responsibilities they had entrusted to me. Now, that responsibility had been heightened with the title "Coach Kiki."

As I continued to reflect, I realized that I had been preparing for this all along. From the moment in high school when my teammates voted for me to be captain of the basketball team, when my classmates selected me as homecoming queen because they believed I would represent them well, and when my teachers frequently recommended me to lead or serve as a spokesperson on behalf of the class or the organization we represented. Later, at junior college, I was selected to be a presidential ambassador, responsible for representing the institution and hosting special guests for the president and board of directors.

All of these activities that happened through high school and college had been preparing me for this type of role: to be a leader—a coach of young women. It was as if I had been positioned for this path all along. It just had not been revealed to me yet. This phenomenon is very common in the lives of those seeking to blaze their own path/trail. And while I wasn't prepared to be a WNBA player, I was most certainly prepared to lead. One of the most important lessons I learned on this journey is that your actions must align with your words. This alignment became clear in the story I shared about needing to change how I showed up when my coach wanted to shift my position, and I had a bad attitude. My mother told me that the problem was me—I needed to adjust my attitude, and then my actions would follow. That lesson was crucial and is now manifesting in a career path I didn't even choose. The beginning of my coaching career marked the culmination of experiences that uniquely prepared me to lead young women.

I understood that it was very important that I had to build and earn their trust. Just because I had been given the title of Coach Kiki, it was no different than when I was selected to be the captain of my teams. The foundational elements I learned from junior high, high school, and college were the same leadership principles that I now applied in a career path that I didn't even select for myself.

APPLYING THE BLIND EXCHANGE FRAMEWORK

- **Faith Gives You Clarity of Vision**

Faith was crucial in helping me see beyond the immediate challenges and uncertainties. The Blind Exchange Framework teaches that faith involves listening and acting without needing to see the outcome. It's about trusting the process and believing that the right path will reveal itself as long as you stay true to your values and instincts. When I received the call from the coach at ULL, it was faith that guided me to explore this new opportunity. Although I had never envisioned myself as a coach, I trusted that this was the direction I was meant to take. My faith gave me the clarity to recognize that the skills I had developed over the years—leadership, communication, and mentorship—were perfectly aligned with this new role.

- **Focus on the Big-Picture Goal**

Focusing on the big-picture goal was another lesson from the Blind Exchange Framework that proved invaluable during this transition. Instead of getting bogged down by the details of whether I would make it in TV or become a coach, I focused on the larger goal of finding a career path that allowed me to utilize my strengths and passions. By keeping my eyes on the broader vision of becoming a leader and making a difference in the lives of others, I was able to navigate the smaller decisions with greater confidence. This focus helped me see that coaching was not just a temporary role but also a stepping stone toward fulfilling my greater purpose.

- **Move Forward to Address Failures Utilizing the Triple-A Method**

Finally, the Forward component of the Blind Exchange Framework emphasized the importance of moving forward despite setbacks. The Triple-A Method—Assess, Acknowledge, and Adjust—became my strategy for dealing with failures and uncertainties during this time.

1. **Assess.** When I faced the choice between continuing with track or pursuing the Communications master's degree, I assessed my circumstances honestly. I recognized that while I had a passion for track, my true calling was in communications and leadership.
2. **Acknowledge.** I acknowledged my imperfections and the fact that I was not fully prepared for either path. However, I also recognized that I had the capacity to grow and learn in this new role as a coach.
3. **Adjust.** With this self-awareness, I adjusted my actions and aligned them with my purpose. I embraced the role of a coach, knowing that it would help me develop the skills and experience I needed to eventually reach my ultimate goals.

As I continued to grow in my role at ULL, I saw how these lessons had shaped my journey. The lessons in faith, focus, and forward momentum were not just abstract concepts; they were practical tools that guided me through one of the most significant transitions in my life. My decision to become a coach was not just about finding a job—it was about discovering a path that allowed me to live out my purpose and make a meaningful impact on the lives of others.

Looking back, I can see how each step I took, each decision I made, was influenced by the foundational lessons I had learned. I had been preparing for this path all along, even if I hadn't realized it at the time. The

Blind Exchange Framework helped me navigate the uncertainty and find clarity in the midst of transition, leading me to a career that I hadn't anticipated but which was perfectly aligned with my strengths and passions.

FORESIGHT AND VISION: THE POWER OF INTENTION

After my very first year of coaching, I said to my mom, "I'm going to be a head coach by the age of 25." This declaration illustrates the power of foresight and intention. This wasn't just a random thought—it was the culmination of years of preparation, experiences, and lessons I had learned along the way. The decision to set such a specific goal shows how my vision was shaped by a deep understanding of my strengths, skills, and the trajectory I was on. This is a prime example of how faith, as part of the Blind Exchange Framework, gives you clarity of vision. Even when the path wasn't entirely clear, my faith in my abilities and the process I was going through allowed me to see beyond the immediate circumstances and set a bold goal for myself.

MY JOURNEY TO HEAD COACH

It is said that hindsight is 20/20. Now I could fully see that I had been preparing for years to walk this path of leading young women. So, I spent two years as a graduate assistant at the University of Louisiana at Lafayette, and I didn't refuse any assignment that I was given. I said yes to all assignments.

- Lead the basketball camp? Yes, I can do that.
- Lead the recruiting efforts? Yes, I can do that.
- Lead player development? Yes, I can do that.

During this time, I also built strong relationships with other coaches on the staff. They became new advisors for me, helping to identify blind spots and fill in the gaps in my knowledge. I learned so much from them. Their guidance was invaluable, allowing me to be more effective in my roles and better prepared for the assignments I was given. This network of support was critical, and it taught me that foresight also involves surrounding yourself with people who can help you see beyond your immediate perspective.

After spending two years as a graduate assistant, I got my first full-time assistant coaching job at Southern University at Baton Rouge (SUBR). It was an opportunity to be full-time, but the coach I went to work for was in the final year of his contract. He was honest with me and said, "I'm in the final year of my contract, and there is a possibility that my contract may not be renewed. So, you may take this opportunity with me and potentially have to be looking for another job at the end of the season."

Another full-time coaching opportunity that had been presented to me would have taken me back to Texas. It was from a former coach from a junior college that I competed against at SPC. He remembered me as a student-athlete and thought I was a fierce competitor. Seeing what I had done now for two years as a graduate assistant, he thought I would be a great addition to his team.

I prayed for direction, assessing both options carefully. Should I take the path with a coach who might have more stability, or should I stick with the one in his final year of contract and see how things unfold? Ultimately, I chose to take the opportunity at Southern because I would be able to continue my master's degree and be close to my support system. This decision was a reflection of the Triple-A Method—*Assess, Acknowledge,* and *Adjust*—that I had learned over time. I assessed my circumstances, acknowledged the risks, and adjusted my plans to align with my long-term goals. Even though this coach only had one year left, I believed that staying put was the right decision given the factors involved.

I was 24 years old and excited about my path now as a leader of young women. That year turned out to be a great learning experience, even though it was challenging. I earned my first full-time salary of $24,500, and I was thrilled to finally say that I was a full-time assistant coach. But the season didn't go as planned, and my head coach's contract wasn't renewed. The athletic director decided to go in a different direction, and because I was still young and relatively inexperienced, I wasn't being considered for the head coaching position. I found myself at another crossroads, needing to figure out my next move.

Then, just as I was contemplating my next steps, I received a call from a friend from home who said, "Hey, Kiki, would you be interested in coming home? There is a head coaching opportunity here at Southern University at Shreveport (SUS), the local junior college, and I told the chancellor that you would be a great fit for that job. If you're interested, he'd love to have an opportunity to connect with you." This was a week or two prior to my 25th birthday. I said, "I'd love the opportunity to have a conversation with the chancellor." The chancellor asked me if I could make a trip home that next week to see the facilities and meet him, the AD, and other pertinent staff to interview for the position.

I remember being very excited for the interview. I showed up, met the chancellor, and we talked about his vision for the program. He was looking for someone young and dynamic. He also thought that there were opportunities within the sports industry for me to get professional development. After meeting with him, the athletic director, other key members, and touring the facilities, he offered me the job of head coach to help rebuild the program. A day or two after my 25th birthday, I was able to say that I had achieved my goal of becoming a head coach by 25. It was an amazing moment, a culmination of all the experiences and lessons that had prepared me for this path.

I was called to lead. I was called to speak and inspire.

As I reflected on this achievement, I realized that I had been preparing for this role all along, even when I didn't consciously recognize it. From being voted captain of my high school basketball team to serving as a presidential ambassador in college, every leadership role I took on was a step toward this moment. The foresight I had—setting the goal to be a head coach by 25—wasn't just about predicting the future, but about trusting the process, focusing on the big picture, and preparing myself for the opportunities that would come my way.

Basketball had been the vehicle that provided me with the opportunity to develop and utilize these specific skills, but the real journey was about discovering my purpose. Even though I didn't end up with a TV show, I was still able to use the communication skills I had developed in my role as a coach. This was a powerful realization: Sometimes, the path you think you're on leads you to an even greater purpose than you originally envisioned.

CONCLUSION

As I look back, it's clear that each step of the journey was about more than just achieving a title or a position. It was about understanding that there is something each of us is naturally good at, something we do so effortlessly that it doesn't even seem extraordinary to us. For me, that was leadership. People had always sought me out to lead, to represent them, to speak on their behalf. This natural inclination was something I had been cultivating all along, and it was now manifesting in a career path that I hadn't initially chosen but was perfectly suited for.

The Blind Exchange Framework was at work throughout this journey. Faith gave me the clarity of vision to set bold goals, Focus helped me to concentrate on the process rather than the immediate results, and Forward Momentum allowed me to navigate the uncertainties and adjust my path as needed. This is what it means to blaze your own trail: not to have every answer from the start, but to be open to the possibilities, prepared for the opportunities, and committed to moving forward no matter what challenges arise.

8
MY PURPOSE REALIZED

Being open to the possibilities and taking those steps helped me start positioning myself for my purpose. The most interesting thing about this journey has been the fact that every time I thought I had the answer, I would realize that this was just the beginning. When I entered the workforce thinking I was preparing myself to finally get on TV, I discovered, *Oh my gosh, no, I am destined to lead young women. I am going to be the coach of the year.* After reading this book, you should know that I believe in being the best, and I want to be at the top. Now that I'm a head coach, I have to be the best head coach. It's not just enough to hold the title; we have to win. I want us to be a winning program, I want to see young women graduate, and I want to see young women (like me) find their purpose. I thought that was all a part of my purpose. So now I'm on my path. I'm excited. I'm walking this path that I believe is the one I have been prepared for, and now I'm positioned for purpose.

One of the things that was really cool about taking on this new head coaching job was that I didn't just take on the head coaching job for basketball. There was also an opportunity to take on the head coaching job for two other programs: the cheer and dance programs.

Now, I've told you all about my love for cheerleading. It was the first thing I wanted to do before I even played basketball and ran track.

I wanted to be a cheerleader first, so, it was very exciting to have this opportunity to be not only a head basketball coach but also the head cheer and dance coach. There were only four athletic programs in the athletic department, and I would be in charge of three.

At the time, I was running those programs simultaneously and doing amazing things. It was such a joy to have the opportunity to do that. It was here that the foundation of a greater purpose started to be laid. I didn't know it then, but being the leader of three out of the four programs was foreshadowing the next stop on my path. It was also the beginning of my first opportunity to look at the athletics industry in its entirety, not just as a coach. I started noticing all these other roles and positions that existed in athletics: there was an athletic director, a sports information director, academic counselors, and business operations administrators. When I was in college, I never really paid attention to any of those other positions and career opportunities in sports.

Being head coach of 75% of the programs, it was interesting to me that the athletic director in charge of all the programs only coached men's basketball. So, in my opinion—using my "girl math," I felt like, *Well, how is he able to be in charge and only have one program while I'm over three out of four programs?* It seemed to me as if it would make more sense for me to be the athletic director since I was basically running all but one of the programs. After about six months, the athletic director position became available. I remember thinking, *I'm finishing my master's degree, I'm running three out of the four programs: I should be the next athletic director.* Unfortunately, the leadership at the institution didn't see it that way. I was a young woman. As I started to examine the industry, I realized that there were very few women leading athletic departments in the country.

And so, it was there that the seed was planted. Maybe if I get tired of coaching at some point, I should become an athletic director.

POSITIONED FOR PURPOSE

This idea stayed in my mind. I thought, *Maybe one day, if I decide that I don't want to coach anymore, I could be an athletic director.* I also remember thinking that if I decided to pursue this path as a young Black woman, I would probably need to have all the titles and degrees. I understood the unique world that we live in, where Black women often experience both racism and sexism.

There was a time when women were considered property and had to fight for the right to vote. We had to fight for the right to have a career. We had to fight for the right to decide what we wanted to do with our own bodies. Understanding all these circumstances made me realize that if I pursued this path, at some point, I would need a PhD and a ton of experience to compete for the opportunity.

But in the meantime, I decided to focus on being the best coach I could be. I remember having the time of my life at SUS. We did some amazing things during my two years there. The dance team and cheer squads had an opportunity to perform on the big stage at the Bayou Classic, the annual football game featuring two Louisiana Historically Black Colleges and Universities, Grambling State University and Southern University at Baton Rouge. The Bayou Classic happens in New Orleans the Saturday following Thanksgiving. It was the first time this opportunity had ever happened. As a coach, I hosted a huge recruitment event that brought in coaches from the region to recruit local student-athletes. It was one of my ways of building relationships. I wanted to become a resource for the small schools in that region. Part of doing that was making myself available to local junior high and high school coaches to help them get their kids recruited. The junior college system was not widely known and accepted in North Louisiana. Because I had the opportunity to attend a junior college, I thought it was important to tell my community at large, "Hey, this is an opportunity." Of course, I couldn't recruit all the players to my school—I only had 15 roster spots—but there were many students who deserved the opportunity to play college ball and get a degree. So it didn't hurt to invite other college coaches to the area to recruit and provide additional opportunities to those young student-athletes.

BUILDING FOR THE FUTURE

There was enough room for everyone to fill their teams. I thought it was important in my role as head coach to become a resource to help kids get into colleges and have their education paid for. It was an amazing opportunity to launch these initiatives, working with communities while I rebuilt the program. Unfortunately, during my two years, there was a lot of instability at the institution. The chancellor who initially hired me left, the athletic director left, and then every semester, I had a different leader. All I could think was that I didn't want to be in an environment where I had a new boss every semester. I started thinking about what would be next for me.

That seed of eventually becoming an athletic director stayed at the back of my mind. I thought, *Maybe this is a good time for me to consider eventually going back to school.* I began to position myself to think about what a move would look like for me. Where would I attend school? I needed a year to transition and understand my next steps. I decided to step down as head coach and took an opportunity as an assistant coach at another junior college, Frank Phillips College (FPC). This role didn't pay much, but it offered me the chance to use another set of skills that I had been developing. In this assistant coaching role, I was offered the opportunity to teach some college courses because I had my master's degree and was qualified to teach. I was allowed to teach a public speaking course because my master's was in communications.

Though I hadn't taught a college course before, I knew how to speak in front of people. I knew how to prepare a practice plan, which is similar to preparing a lesson plan for a class. It was no different from when my coach met with me and gave me templates to use when I first started as a graduate assistant coach. When I met with the dean, he gave me a template for a curriculum and lesson plan that I would implement for my classes. I had the opportunity to adjust those templates and make them more relevant to my classes. The same lessons I learned from coaching and developing practice plans had equipped me to develop lesson plans for my courses.

THE POWER OF SAYING YES

As the position was not full-time, they couldn't pay me a full salary, but they offered me free housing if I agreed to be a dorm mom. Now, I had never managed a dorm before, but I had coached young student-athletes and was responsible for making sure they were in their rooms and had schedules on the road. Running an entire dorm was similar to managing three out of four athletic programs. Instead of just being in charge of a few student-athletes on three programs, I was now responsible for many students who lived in the dorm. The processes for how students got a dorm room and community conduct guidelines were already laid out. Surely, if I could concurrently lead a college cheer program, a college dance program, and a college basketball program, I could manage a dorm.

I spent one year at this institution, expanding my skill set. Leading a full dorm and teaching courses added more skills to my toolkit. It reminded me of my freshman year when my coach wanted me to transition to point guard and learn new skills, and I said no. I knew the only appropriate response was YES.

When I was asked to run the dorm, teach courses, and be an assistant coach, I continued to say YES. At SUS, when I was asked to be the cheer and dance coach, I said YES. Saying yes to these opportunities allowed me to continue developing my leadership skills and to learn and work with broader groups of people across the college campus.

This transition year was preparing and positioning me for my next chapter. After I finished that year at Frank Phillips College as the dorm director, instructor, and coach, I began to visualize myself leading an athletic department. I decided it was time to get a PhD. As I said in Chapter 7, as a Black woman, I would need all the credentials to be considered for an athletic director position. At least that's the way I saw it.

MOVING FORWARD WITH PURPOSE

I decided, *Why not go back to a familiar place?* I returned to New Orleans, where I had professors who still supported me. I had mentors there, and I told them, "I would love to come back here and consider a PhD program in higher education." There were two programs available: a counseling program and a higher education administration program.

In my roles as a coach and dorm director, students often sought my advice. They would ask, "Can I talk to you about a situation?" and seek my counsel and advice. I initially thought that counseling was the PhD program to pursue.

I thought counseling would be great. This would be a way to merge all of these skills I'd learned as a head coach and dorm director, which would make me a more attractive athletic director candidate as I continued on this path. This was my first and only year off from working in an athletics department in my entire career. I began my PhD journey with acceptance into the counseling program.

Now I didn't have a job. I was enrolling in this doctoral program at the age of 28 as a full-time student. Because I didn't have a job, I had to move into the dorm. My roommate was 18 years old, and I remember thinking, *Am I really starting over again?* While it felt odd, I knew this was the right move. I knew this was what I needed to do, but I wasn't quite sure how it would all work out. Getting accepted into the program was helpful. I had applied for an assistantship, and if I could get it, maybe I could move to graduate student housing. I remembered being in the dorm and visiting my coach, who wanted me to catch him up on everything I had done for the past few years. I explained that I had become a head coach at 25, coached cheer and dance, and spent the last year at a junior college teaching courses, coaching, and managing the dorm. He said, "Oh, you managed the dorm? My buddy who runs the management company for the dorm you're living in is looking for a residential hall coordinator. Would you be interested?"

I met with him, and after one semester in the dorm, I was the new dorm director. All I could think was, *What if I had done what I did my freshman year in college when my coach told me I should be a point guard? What if I had said no to the dorm director job at my previous employer?* If I hadn't said yes to being the dorm director, my coach wouldn't have thought to mention my name to his colleague. This shows the importance of saying yes and not closing yourself off to opportunities. What you see as extra work is preparation and positioning for the next step on your unique path. I went from not having a job to being in charge of the dorm, getting free housing and meals, and an $18,000 yearly stipend.

While it wasn't a lot of money, I didn't have any living expenses, so I got to keep all of it. It helped me stay focused on my PhD pursuit. As I contemplated what was next, I knew I was positioning myself to be an athletic director. I figured that after I got my PhD, I'd work in an athletic department for 15 to 20 years, and maybe, by 50 or so, I'd have enough experience to compete for an athletic director position. I was enjoying the counseling courses, but I realized this wasn't in alignment with my skills and abilities. I tell people what to do. As a coach, I directed people.

As a dorm director, I instructed, implemented policies, and established systems to help us operate efficiently and effectively. I couldn't imagine being in a role where I just had to listen and couldn't provide solutions. As I continued through the program, I realized the counseling degree wasn't aligned with my gifts to direct, build, instruct, create systems, and lead. I spoke with my professor, and we decided the best course was to transition from the counseling program to the higher education administration program. Administrators lead, direct, provide counsel, create systems, and make things happen. My experiences as a coach, teacher, and dorm director suited me more for an administrative role than a counseling role. The beautiful thing was that the counseling courses I had taken helped me fine-tune my listening skills, a key foundational element of blazing your own trail. Improving my listening skills was crucial as I continued to develop my leadership skills and focused on research in higher education administration. The counseling courses counted as electives in my doctoral program, so I didn't lose any progress toward my degree.

POSITIONED ON PURPOSE, FOR A PURPOSE

As the transition was happening, Dillard University, which was literally a mile from the University of New Orleans, had just named Robin Martin (now Dr. Robin Martin), its first female athletic director. As fate would have it, she was also a graduate of the University of New Orleans and a former player and assistant women's basketball coach there. I transferred to UNO in August 1995, as Robin left to become a head girls' basketball coach at a local high school. I had heard stories about her from other players and how amazing she was as a coach. She would even come and watch us play.

I developed a relationship with her, and I was so excited because I had said that, at some point in my career, maybe I'd be an athletic director. I called her to congratulate her and tell her how proud I was of her new role as athletic director. As we continued our conversation, she asked, "What have you been doing since you left UNO?"

So, I told her my story: head coach by 25, coach, cheer, dance, dorm director. As we talked, she said, "You know, I'm looking for a cheer coach." I was happy being the dorm director and pursuing my degree full-time, so I didn't think there was any way I was going to be the cheer coach at Dillard.

She was proud of my work and said, "I'll circle back with you in a week or so, and let's talk more about this opportunity."

She called back a week later and said she was starting to have doubts about the person to whom she'd initially offered the assistant coaching job, and that person might not accept it. I told her I was concerned about fulfilling my dorm director duties and coaching because my dorm director role required me to be on call 24/7. I hadn't figured out how I could be on call and coach at the same time. I said I needed more time to think about it. She said, "Okay, I'll call you back at the end of the week for your final answer."

I have to say, telling Robin Martin no was probably never going to be an option, but I just didn't see how I'd be able to fulfill my dorm obligations and be the cheer coach. When she called back, she said, "I know I talked to you about the cheer position, but the assistant coaching position is now available, and I really want to offer it to you.

It's a full-time position. You'll be making $38,000." I remember thinking that was the most money I had ever been offered. It would give me the chance to be the number two person reporting directly to the athletic director.

So now I had two paths in front of me: to get back into coaching and work directly for an athletic director, or to continue my academic career, stay in student affairs, work as a dorm director, and consider a path toward becoming a president. I thought, *I've done sports all my life. I love sports. I know sports. I said I wanted to be an athletic director, and what better way to learn this role than to work directly with an athletic director?* I said my prayers, reflected as always, and paid attention to what was happening in my life. I talked to some trusted advisors and ultimately decided that becoming the full-time assistant coach was the right path. I remember taking that role and being super excited to not only have the support of a strong Black woman who valued me and thought I had a lot to offer, but also to learn from one of the best. What better way to do this than under her leadership? As I reflected on this opportunity, I kept thinking about how each step of this path was positioning me for the purpose that was starting to reveal itself.

If I hadn't taken the dorm director job, would I have been the dorm director at UNO if I hadn't said yes to the opportunity the year before? If the coach had not left and the athletic director position had not become available, would I have even considered being an athletic director if I hadn't been denied that opportunity?

All these thoughts crossed my mind as I reflected on the opportunity to join Robin as her assistant. She would be a mentor and guide for me. It was a chance to study with someone who was leading as an athletic director. I kept thinking, *What if I hadn't said yes to being the cheer, dance, and women's basketball coach? What if I hadn't said yes to being the dorm director and the teacher at Frank Phillips College?*

Those were the opportunities that set off a chain of events that led me to Dillard University as an assistant under someone who would lead and help me think about and understand what my role as an athletic director might look like. I was excited to work for the first woman athletic director. We completed our first year, and it was exciting.

So many amazing things happened there. I met my soon-to-be husband, Marc A. Barnes, three days after my 30th birthday. I met him in April, and we were engaged on June 3, 2005. On July 8, 2005, his father passed away. On August 29, 2005, Hurricane Katrina hit New Orleans and decimated the city. On October 31, I was laid off from Dillard University.

I remember being devastated by what was happening. They had to let go of at least 50 percent of the workforce because the hurricane had prevented us from having a semester, which meant no tuition revenue and, therefore, no money with which to pay staff. I was upset because I felt I had made the right decision and was on the right path. I had said my prayers, reflected on everything, and it was clear that I was supposed to take this opportunity to work with Robin. To have this taken away from me made me question whether I had made the right decision, whether I was on the right path, and whether all these things I thought had positioned me were pointing me in the right direction. While I continued my academic career, I slipped into a small depression about this opportunity being taken away.

Marc and I decided to move up our wedding, and we secretly got married on November 12, 2005. We planned to come back and live together, so we wanted to be in good standing both spiritually and morally, especially since he had two children who would be impacted by this. We moved back to New Orleans in January 2006 and lived in the Marriott Hotel on Canal Street for six months while figuring out how to navigate and rebuild in the city. Luckily, Marc was still employed by Dillard University.

One day, Marc came home and shared that he had heard Robin would be taking on another role as athletic director at an institution in California. Dillard's new president faced the decision of who would replace her. It was a very tumultuous time, as the university operated out of the Hilton Hotel on the Riverfront, and some staff shared office space with Tulane University downtown while the administration figured out how to get the university up and running again. As part of the cuts, they had reduced the athletics programs to only three: men's and women's basketball and volleyball. Marc said, "My boss wanted to know if you would be interested in being the women's basketball coach since you were her assistant."

"I'd love to be the head coach if I could also be the athletic director."

He said, "I'll let him know, and we'll see what happens." So, my husband shared this with his boss, and eventually, his boss connected me with the person responsible for hiring.

As I prepared for the interview process, I thought about how I could communicate that I was the right person to hire despite not having been an athletic director.

Reflecting during my interview preparation, I remembered my first head coaching job and how I managed three out of the four programs. Dillard University only had three programs. While I had not been an athletic director, I felt that if I could manage three programs at my previous school, then I could manage three programs here. I had also run an entire dorm at two separate institutions, a community college, and a large four-year public university. My experience showed that I could manage a large group of people. So, even though I had not held the title of athletic director, I was perfectly positioned and prepared for this path at this moment.

During my interview, I spoke confidently about my experiences and the things I had done as a leader. I wanted to address the title issue head-on and said, "I know I have not been an athletic director, but I have proven that I can lead multiple programs. I was the head coach of three out of four programs during my time at Southern University at Shreveport."

I was offered the athletic director and head women's basketball coaching position at Dillard University in August 2006, giving me the opportunity of a lifetime to rebuild an athletic program. What I will say to you is this: if you are open to the possibilities in your life, the things that have been waiting for you, you have already been preparing for and are already prepared for those opportunities. As I continue to reflect on those experiences from middle school all the way through college, every experience and opportunity led me to this point: being named athletic director at 31 years old, tasked with leading a program after a natural disaster. I was made for a time such as this. I was positioned on purpose, for a purpose, and the same can happen for you.

CONCLUSION

I have shared my stories in this book to show you how I arrived at the beginning of my career, each step guided by faith, focus, and forward momentum. Every challenge, every "yes," and every pivot has positioned me on purpose, for a purpose. But this journey is far from over—it's still unfolding. My path may not be the same as yours, but the lessons in resilience, preparation, and trusting the process apply to every journey. As you reflect on what you've read, I encourage you to think about your own path. These are my stories—what are yours? How can you apply the Blind Exchange Framework to your life? How will you allow faith, focus, and forward momentum to guide your next step? The power to shape your future lies within you, and your next chapter is waiting to be written.

CONCLUSION: A NEW BEGINNING

What an incredible journey this has been. I am so excited that I've had the opportunity to share a small part of my journey with you. I want to point out a few things and remind you of what you need to think about.

At the end of the day, we're always solving for X. You can never know everything, and guess what? That is absolutely okay because you don't have to know everything. But here are the things that you *do* need to know.

You don't really lose—you learn. That's what this is all about. When you put things in the right perspective, a loss can turn into an opportunity for learning. We also talk specifically about being focused on the process. Even the process of writing this book has been so much fun. I have enjoyed the opportunity to reflect on all of the things that I've experienced step by step, starting with an outline and then adding points under those, finding stories that align with each point. Every part of the process of writing this book is no different than the process that you read about as I was developing my leadership, becoming a better coach, and becoming a better leader. Focusing on the process is a fundamental pillar of leadership.

Momentum is established when we move forward toward the goal.

You can't move forward if you are standing still. It's really important that as you're embracing the process, you're focusing on taking the action steps that will lead you closer to your goal. Being open to feedback is crucial. Remember the heartbreaking story of me not getting the WNBA opportunity because I wasn't open to doing something different? Learning a new skill in college was a heartbreaking yet important lesson: you never know what opportunities will exist for your next steps. Embracing preparation is key. When you don't know what's going to happen and when you can't determine which step to take next, preparation will give you the foresight to see beyond your present circumstances. If you recall, I graduated from college saying I wanted to work in a TV studio or in media, but I wasn't prepared to do that. As I was faced with a pivotal decision about which road to take, I took the one that I was clearly prepared for. And guess what? You are being prepared too. Embracing preparation is a critical part of blazing your own trail and fully realizing your own power.

OWNING YOUR POWER: BLAZING YOUR OWN TRAIL

Owning your power is the final step needed to blaze your own trail. Owning your power is a mindset focused on taking decisive action towards your purpose. When you make up your mind to take ownership of your abilities and decisions, you are aligning with the unique talents, skills, passions, desires, and dreams that were given to you to make a difference in this world. Foresight and failure both serve as catalysts to cultivate the resilience and determination required to navigate the twists and turns of your journey with confidence. So don't be afraid. Take action today and say yes to your challenges and to your purpose. Spend time reflecting on those advisors who have invested in your success and take advantage of that. Thank them for being invested in you. These are all great action steps that you can take right now to get it done.

Because at the end of the day, guess what? The most exciting part of all of this is that you have the power to change direction at any moment. And that's the good news. All you have to do is decide. No one can decide for you—not your mom, your dad, your sister, your brother, teachers, counselors, or supervisors. No one but you can make the decision for you.

Moreover, owning your power encourages you to embrace your individuality. Your path is distinct, shaped by your own experiences and insights. When you own your power, you are more likely to celebrate your uniqueness and draw from it as a source of strength. This not only enhances your journey but also inspires others to do the same, creating a community of trailblazers who support and uplift one another.

Much of what I learned about blazing my own trail, I learned through sports. As I reflected on my more than 20-year career in sports, I began to realize what a travesty it was that I had not even considered a career in athletics, despite being an active participant in sports since 5th grade. Coupled with being the only woman athletic director out of 24 in the state of Louisiana for at least a decade, I recognized that there was a gap, and my path had uniquely prepared me to address it.

I started a program called "So You Want a Career in Athletics," a professional development initiative of the Marc and Kiki Barnes Foundation, which invests in girls and young women through educational programming. The mission of SYWACIA™ is to strengthen the pipeline of female leaders in sports by educating girls and young women on leadership and career opportunities. Our annual programs include interactive webinars and in-person events such as the SYWACIA™ Sports Leadership Academy and our annual National Girls & Women's in Sports Day event collaborations. You can get connected to a community of women by visiting our website, www.sywacia.com, and signing up for our newsletter.

Ultimately, owning your power is about embracing the responsibility that comes with it. It means acknowledging that you have the ability to influence your destiny and make meaningful contributions to the world. By owning your power, you are not just blazing your own trail; you are setting an example for others to follow, encouraging them to take ownership of their journeys as well.

This book has brought me to this point, reflecting on the lessons learned, the challenges faced, and the victories earned along the way.

But this is not the end—this is just the beginning. The real journey starts now, and the path ahead is mine to create. With every step forward, new possibilities unfold. And so, I invite you to do the same: embrace your power, trust your process, and blaze your trail. The journey is waiting—let's begin.

THANK YOU FOR READING MY BOOK!

DOWNLOAD YOUR FREE Trailblazing Action Plan

Just to say thanks for buying and reading my book, I would like to give you a free bonus gift, no strings attached!

TO DOWNLOAD NOW, VISIT:

I appreciate your interest in my book and value your feedback as it helps me improve future versions of this book. I would appreciate it if you could leave your invaluable review on Amazon.com with your feedback.
Thank you!

www.ingramcontent.com/pod-product-compliance
Lightning Source LLC
Chambersburg PA
CBHW050243010526
44107CB00032B/1388/J